The Land and People of

NORWAY

The Land and People of ®
NORWAY

by Claudette Charbonneau and Patricia Slade Lander

Special photographs by Ola Røe

HarperCollins*Publishers*

Country maps by Robert Romagnoli
Every effort has been made to locate the copyright holders of all copyrighted materials and to secure the necessary permission to reproduce them. In the event of any questions arising as to their use, the publisher will be glad to make necessary changes in future printings and editions.
The map on page 144 is taken from *Norway and the Second World War*, by John Andenaes and O. Riste (H. Aschehoug & Co., Oslo, 1989), by permission.
The poem on page 30 is quoted from *News from the Top of the World: Norwegian Literature Today* (Oslo, 1988). Reprinted by permission of Harald Gaski, translator.
The poem on pages 74–75 is quoted from *Peter Dass: The Trumpet of Nordland,* translated and edited by Theodore Jorgensen (Northfield, Minn.: St. Olaf College Press, 1954). Reprinted by permission of the publisher.
The poem on page 177 is quoted from *Norway Information*, April 1986, Royal Norwegian Ministry of Foreign Affairs, UDA 503 ENG. Reprinted by permission.

The Land and People of Norway
Copyright © 1992 by Claudette Charbonneau and Patricia Slade Lander
Printed in the U.S.A. All rights reserved.
For information address HarperCollins Children's Books,
a division of HarperCollins Publishers,
10 East 53rd Street, New York, NY 10022.

Library of Congress Cataloging-in-Publication Data
Charbonneau, Claudette, date
      The land and people of Norway / by Claudette Charbonneau
and Patricia Slade Lander ; special photographs by Ola Røe.
          p.   cm.   —   (Portraits of the nations)
      Includes bibliographical references (p.) and index.
      Filmography: p.
      Summary: Introduces the history, geography, people, culture,
government, and economy of Norway.
      ISBN 0-06-020573-3. — ISBN 0-06-020583-0 (lib. bdg.)
      1. Norway—Juvenile literature. [1. Norway.] I. Lander,
Patricia Slade.   II. Title.   III. Series.
DL409.C43   1992   91-35029
948.1—dc20   CIP
                                                              AC

1   2   3   4   5   6   7   8   9   10
First Edition

ACKNOWLEDGMENTS

This book would never have even been started without the encouraging support of Odd Wibe, Director of the Norwegian Information Service in New York (now Norwegian Ambassador to Kuwait), who understands well the importance of intercultural communication.

In Norway, we were impressed by the helpfulness of people in the North who communicated the specialness of that area, especially Arne Christian Vangdal, as well as Ericka Engelstad, Åse Hiorth Lervik, May Britt Manin, and Marit Myrvoll (Sami Secretariat). Anne Larsen, along with Anne Berg, Marianne Gullestad, Michael Jones, and Bente Rasmussen of various research departments in Trondheim and Tove Søreide of the Nidaros Cathedral, as well as Svein Knutsen, Kari Øie, and Solveig Isabel Taylor gave us many valuable insights. Inger Munch-Ellingsen, Torbjørn Nervik, and Anne Torsvik shared their knowledge of Rogaland's rich history, while Svein Brekke of Morgedal, ski historian Helvor Kleppen, and Lisbet Sauarlia explained the customs of Telemark and the Norwegian contribution to skiing.

Among others in Oslo, we wish to thank David Arnett, Helga Braein, Janicke Bye, Stein Fredriksen, Ragnhild Galtung, Vegard Halvorsen, Johan Heyerdahl, Kristin Hobson, Eiliv Hoibakken, Magnar Hovde, May-Britt Lund, Matte Oewre, Tove Beate Pedersen, Trine Tandberg, Peter Udbjørg, Leong Vá, Valborg Vigsnes, Long Litt Woon, and Per Paust of the Royal Norwegian Ministry of Foreign Affairs (who made us wonder whether Christopher Columbus could have been a Norwegian!). Throughout Norway, the helpfulness of many museum guides, hoteliers, and people on the street—whose names we never learned—is remembered with fondness.

In New York, Harald Hansen (Norwegian Tourist Board); Kari Hovik, Gerd Petersen, Astrid Raad Tabatabai, and Irene Varvayanis (Norwegian Information Service); Gerd Bjorgan (Kon-Tiki Travel Service, Brooklyn); and Margaret and William Lander made our work easier. Finally, we wish to thank our editor, Marc Aronson, whose intelligence and even-temperedness, even in times of stress, made it possible for us to write this book.

To all, tusen takk!

Contents

THE WORLD

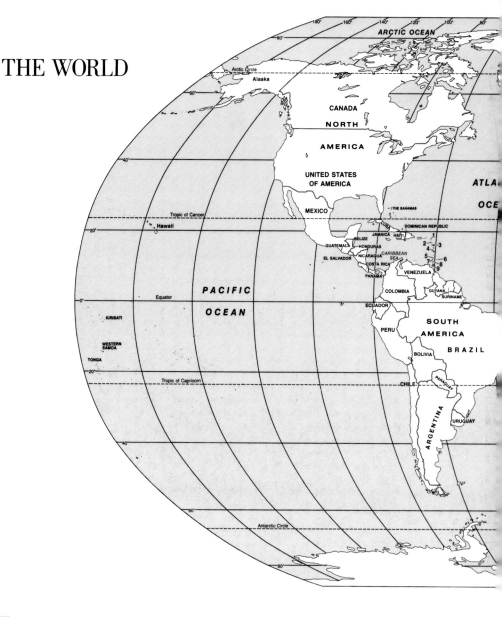

This world map is based on a projection developed by Arthur H. Robinson. The shape of each country and its size, relative to other countries, are more accurately expressed here than in previous maps. The map also gives equal importance to all of the continents, instead of placing North America at the center of the world. *Used by permission of the Foreign Policy Association.*

Legend

―――― International boundaries

--------- Disputed or undefined boundaries

Projection: Robinson

0	1000	2000	3000 Miles

0	1000	2000	3000 Kilometers

Caribbean Nations

1. Anguilla
2. St. Christopher and Nevis
3. Antigua and Barbuda
4. Dominica
5. St. Lucia
6. Barbados
7. St. Vincent
8. Grenada
9. Trinidad and Tobago

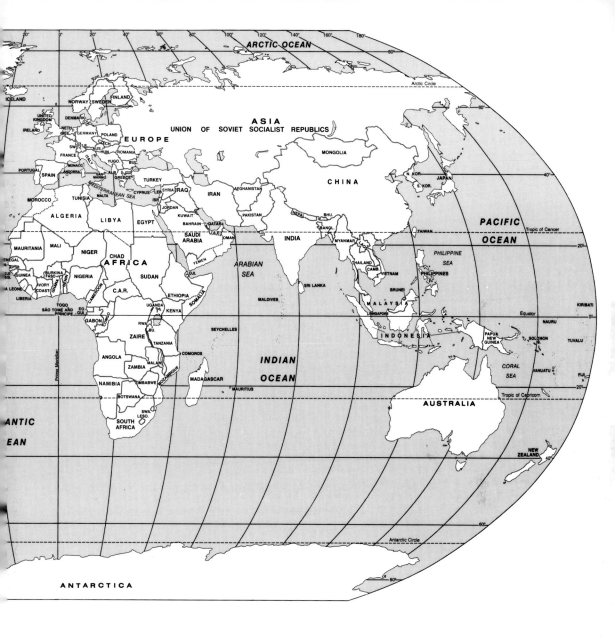

Abbreviations

ALB.	—Albania	C.A.R.	—Central African Republic	LEB.	—Lebanon	SWA.	—Swaziland
AUS.	—Austria	CZECH.	—Czechoslovakia	LESO.	—Lesotho	SWITZ.	—Switzerland
BANGL.	—Bangladesh	DJI.	—Djibouti	LIE.	—Liechtenstein	U.A.E.	—United Arab Emirates
BEL.	—Belgium	EQ. GUI.	—Equatorial Guinea	LUX.	—Luxemburg	YUGO.	—Yugoslavia
BHU.	—Bhutan	GER.	Germany	NETH.	—Netherlands		
BU.	—Burundi	GUI. BIS.	—Guinea Bissau	N. KOR.	—North Korea		
BUL.	—Bulgaria	HUN.	—Hungary	RWA.	—Rwanda		
CAMB.	—Cambodia	ISR.	—Israel	S. KOR.	—South Korea		

Mini Facts

OFFICIAL NAME: The Kingdom of Norway (in Norwegian, *Kongeriket Norge*)

LOCATION: Mainland Norway lies in the western portion of the Scandinavian peninsula in northern Europe between 57° 57' 31" and 71° 77' 8" north latitude. Norway is surrounded by seas on three sides. To the south and southwest is the North Sea; to the west, the Norwegian Sea of the North Atlantic Ocean; and to the north, the Barents Sea of the Arctic Ocean. In the east, Norway has common borders with Sweden of 1,044 miles (1,680 kilometers), with Finland of 447 mi. (719 km.), and with the Russian Republic of 122 mi. (196 km.). Denmark lies to the south across the Skagerrak Channel, an arm of the North Sea, and Scotland to the southwest across the North Sea.

AREA: Norway's total area is 149,366 square miles or 386,658 square kilometers. Mainland Norway is slightly larger than New Mexico, with 125,017 sq. mi. or 323,794 sq. km.. Svalbard, a group of islands in the Arctic Ocean, is 24,202 sq. mi. or 62,683 sq. km.; the northern island of Jan Mayen is 147 sq. mi. or 371 sq. km. Territories in the Antarctic include Bouvet Island (22.5 sq. mi., 58.3 sq. km.), Peter I Island (96.2 sq. mi., 249.2 sq. km.), and Queen Maud Land, a large expanse of Antarctic coast between 45°E and 20°W longitude.

CAPITAL: Oslo

POPULATION: 4.2 million (1990)

MAJOR LANGUAGES: Norwegian (Bokmål and Nynorsk)

RELIGION: Church of Norway (Evangelical Lutheran)

TYPE OF GOVERNMENT: Hereditary constitutional monarchy with full parliamentary democracy

HEAD OF STATE: Executive power is vested formally in the monarch.

HEAD OF GOVERNMENT: Prime Minister

PARLIAMENT: The Storting is a 165-seat parliament; elections are held every four years.

ADULT LITERACY: 99 percent

LIFE EXPECTANCY: Female, 79.6; Male, 72.9 years

MAIN PRODUCTS: Crude oil, natural gas, metals, pulp and paper, ships, machinery, fish and fish products, chemicals. Two thirds of Norway's exports go to the European Community countries.

CURRENCY: *krone*

Norway: Top of Europe

Norway sits at the top of Europe, which affects everything about the country from the angle of the sun to the routes of the Vikings, from the annual rounds of nomadic reindeer herders to changing defense strategies. Almost half the length of the country lies north of the Arctic Circle (latitude 66° 33'). Curving over Sweden and Finland, Norway meets the Russian Republic near Kirkenes, forming a northern corridor along the Barents Sea at the very edge of the Scandinavian peninsula. In the west Norway is bounded by the Norwegian Sea of the North Atlantic, to the southwest by the North Sea, and in the south by the Skagerrak Channel.

Norway is a strangely shaped country, very long and narrow, with bulges at both ends. Its outline has been compared to fishbones; a tad-

pole with a crooked, irregular tail; an ancient ski; a bumpy squash; or an arrow pointing north. The country is so thin in the middle that at one point it is only 3.9 miles (6.3 kilometers) wide. Mainland Norway spans a distance of over 13° latitude, making it the longest, as well as the narrowest, country in Europe.

Much earlier in geological time Scotland and Norway were united by a common mountain range called the Caledonian fold, made up of granite and porphyry, a rock consisting of crystals in a red or purple ground mass. These rocks date from between one and two billion years ago. A part of this range eventually sank below the sea, and Scotland and Norway separated. The coastline of Norway, however, still looks like a massive sloping barrier of rocks jutting up from the sea, and the belt of rocks and islands lining the coast today is actually peaks of this ancient volcanic mountain range.

No one has made an exact count, but there are approximately 150,000 islands and islets that stand like sentinels facing west, protecting the Norwegian shore from the battering of the stormy seas and extremely strong winds. Many small islands have been home to settlers since prehistoric times, including the Lofoten Islands, near the Arctic Circle, which look like a dragon's back tilting southwestward some 80 mi. (130 km.) into the Norwegian Sea.

The multitude of islands protects the mainland so well that from very ancient times people have been able to sail inside the archipelagoes. The term Norway (*Norge* in Norwegian) comes from the Old Norse word *Nordvegr*, which means the "way to the north," referring to the Viking route along the long coast. The islands form a "corridor"

Norway has been called "the national park of Europe" because of its forests, mountains, glaciers, fjords, and many lakes. Lake Gjende is in the Jotunheimen Mountains.
Norwegian Tourist Board, New York

along the coast that the Norwegians call *Leden*, literally "the lead," a passageway that leads the ships behind the island shield.

White Coal

Memories of the Ice Ages linger in this northern land in the many ice fields on high peaks in the major mountain chain, both north and south of the Arctic Circle. The largest glacier in continental Europe, the Jostedalsbre (*bre* means glacier), is a 320-sq.-mi. (830-sq.-km.) expanse of ice that branches out in many directions, ending at the edges of fjords, farms, and villages in southern Norway.

The glaciers, which began to melt around 12,000 years ago, carved the ancient bedrock and dug out broad U-shaped valleys below vertical rock faces. Today the meltwaters from the surviving glaciers and annual snowfalls pour down the steep slopes in countless waterfalls. These roaring mountain waters have been called Norway's "white coal," since they provide its immense resources of inexpensive hydroelectric power.

Mountains: Symbol of Norway

Norway is one of the most mountainous countries in Europe. The ranges extend almost its entire length, and many painters and writers have used the mountains as a symbol of the country. The glaciers shaped the peaks into such odd forms that they have provoked images of trolls and other supernatural spirits. The mountains in the south, which contain the highest summits in Europe north of the Alps, are called Jotunheimen, "home of the giants." A few mountains are so steep that no climber has ever attempted to scale them, while others have only been attempted in recent years. The 2,000-foot (608-meter)

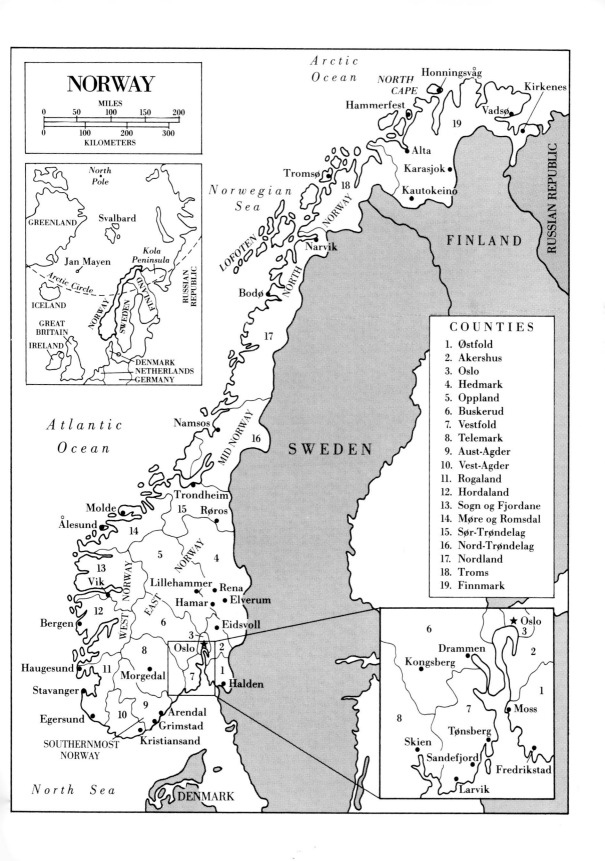

NORWAY

Arctic Ocean

NORTH CAPE
Honningsvåg
Hammerfest
Kirkenes
Vadsø
19
Alta
Karasjok
Kautokeino

North Pole

GREENLAND
Svalbard

Jan Mayen
Kola Peninsula

Arctic Circle

ICELAND

NORWAY
SWEDEN
FINLAND

RUSSIAN REPUBLIC

GREAT BRITAIN

IRELAND

DENMARK
NETHERLANDS
GERMANY

Norwegian Sea

Tromsø
18
NORTH NORWAY
Narvik

LOFOTEN

Bodø
NORTH
17

FINLAND

RUSSIAN REPUBLIC

Atlantic Ocean

Namsos
MID NORWAY
16
SWEDEN

Trondheim
15
Røros
Molde
Ålesund
14
5
NORWAY
4
13
Vik
WEST NORWAY
EAST NORWAY
Lillehammer
Rena
Hamar
Elverum
6
Eidsvoll
12
Bergen
3
Oslo
2
8
Haugesund
11
Morgedal
1
7
Halden
Stavanger
9
Egersund
10
Arendal
Grimstad
Kristiansand
SOUTHERNMOST NORWAY

North Sea

DENMARK

COUNTIES

1. Østfold
2. Akershus
3. Oslo
4. Hedmark
5. Oppland
6. Buskerud
7. Vestfold
8. Telemark
9. Aust-Agder
10. Vest-Agder
11. Rogaland
12. Hordaland
13. Sogn og Fjordane
14. Møre og Romsdal
15. Sør-Trøndelag
16. Nord-Trøndelag
17. Nordland
18. Troms
19. Finnmark

6
Oslo
3
Drammen
2
Kongsberg
1
Moss
8
7
Tønsberg
Skien
Sandefjord
Fredrikstad
Larvik

Reka in Vesterålen in North Norway has never been climbed. The Troll Wall in the county of Møre og Romsdal was first climbed only in 1967, and it has been besieged by rock climbers ever since. Some consider it Europe's most demanding precipice.

The retreating glaciers cut some mountains down into *vidder* (mountain plateaus); others were eroded down to flat plateaus called *fjell* by the weight of the vast ice sheet, which was one and a quarter miles (two kilometers) thick. The most impressive results of glacial erosion in the uplands are the fjords of western Norway. These are very deep and narrow inlets of sea inserted between steep cliffs. The fjords are sometimes even deeper than the North Sea, though they are often shallower near the coast, where the ice sheet was thinner.

Danger Amidst Beauty

Norway's geological foundations are still adjusting, sometimes with such energy that W.R. Mead, a distinguished British geographer, terms Norway "a country characterised by physical catastrophe." Rock slides, snow avalanches, and clay slides constantly modify terraces and intrude on farmlands. The continual erosion of the lands and glaciers is accompanied by noises so unnerving that they were often attributed to the supernatural.

Norwegians have had to make peace with nature to survive. Rather than becoming cautious, though, many have taken great risks beyond their shores in ships around the world and on skis across Greenland and the South Pole. At home Norwegian engineers have devised ways to overcome the heights and depths, stringing high wires across steep gorges and laying gas pipes across the very deep off-shore Norwegian trench, a feat many believed was not possible. Norwegians express their closeness to nature in Sunday walks or skiing treks, in Easter outings to soak up the sun, and in visits to summer cottages or boat docks.

Jumping the Norwegian Trench

Since World War II there have been international debates concerning the definition and use of each nation's continental shelf. These discussions deal with the rights to harvest shellfish and to exploit mineral resources.

Norway has a deep trench about 11 nautical miles (20 kilometers) from the coast. Beyond the trench, the continental shelf continues to stretch toward the coast of Great Britain. At first the British argued that Norway should use only the area up to the trench. Norway claimed that the trench was only an accidental depression.

Eventually the British accepted the Norwegian view. An agreement was signed on March 10, 1965, fixing a boundary 359 nautical miles (665 kilometers) long at a line equidistant between the British and Norwegian coasts.

This agreement gave Norway jurisdiction over ocean areas four times larger than its land area. No other European nation controls such a large continental shelf. The significance of this area grew immensely with the discovery of oil and natural gas fields in the North Sea in December 1969. Schoolchildren used to learn that "nature made Norway a poor country." After the 1965 agreement—and the discovery of oil—this "truth" was quickly outdated.

After most of the glacial cover had melted away, Norway was left with barren lands, rocks, and many lakes covering 74 percent of the country. Forests and woodlands cover another 23 percent, leaving only 3 percent of the land arable, with a thin and rocky soil. Apart from the tiny states of Andorra and Monaco, in all of Europe only neighboring Iceland has a smaller percentage of arable land than Norway. Under-

Svalbard—The Cold Coasts

Svalbard, which means "the cold coasts" in Norwegian, is a chain of four large and several small islands of rugged peaks and fjords, situated about 700 mi. (1,100 km.) from the North Pole. The southern tip of Spitsbergen, the main island, is 350 mi. (563 km.) from North Norway.

On these frozen islands there are no ordinary trees or bushes. Two thirds of the 23,598 sq. mi. (61,119 sq. km.) are covered with glaciers. The ground is permanently frozen to depths that vary from 300 to 1,600 feet (100–500 meters).

About half the area is a nature preserve, with very strict limitations on what people can do there. Some 3,700 people (two thirds of whom are citizens of the former Soviet republics) live on Svalbard with 4,000 to 6,000 polar bears, 10,000 Svalbard reindeer, and arctic foxes and grouse. There are scientific facilities, such as the Norwegian Polar Research Institute, and a new international radar center to study the northern lights will be functioning by 1995 or 1996.

The Vikings probably visited Svalbard, but they thought it was part of Greenland, so the "discovery" is usually dated from 1596, when the Dutch navigator William Barents came upon the uninhabited islands and named them Spitsbergen (pointed hills).

Starting in the early seventeenth century, the islands were used as

ground there are—mostly in the north—modest mineral resources such as silver and copper, iron ore, pyrites, zinc, titanium, antimony, and nickel. Norway's only coal deposits lie in Svalbard.

In spite of the overwhelming presence of mountains and rocks, animals and people have found creative ways to adapt to this spectacularly beautiful but harsh environment. Countless birds—including

bases for whalers and seal hunters of many nations. Coal deposits were found at the beginning of the twentieth century. Currently only a Norwegian state-owned mine and a Russian mine are in operation, neither of which makes a profit. Most analysts believe the real reason that each country keeps a mine open is Svalbard's strategic importance for military maneuvers and future oil exploration.

Treaty of Svalbard

A special commission at the Paris peace conference after World War I crafted a treaty (signed by Norway on February 9, 1920, and ratified in 1925) that granted Norway sovereignty over Svalbard but with the stipulation that it be a demilitarized zone and that all those countries that signed the Treaty of Svalbard, now numbering forty countries, should have economic access to the islands' natural resources.

The isolation of Svalbard is decreasing steadily. An airport was opened in the town of Longyearbyen, the administrative capital, in 1975. Planes from Tromsø arrive about twice a week, and about once a month from Moscow. Telephone communication to the Norwegian mainland via satellite has existed since 1979 and television from Norway since 1984. In the early 1980's Norwegian television began to include Svalbard's weather in the regular weather report.

Until 1966 the governor of Svalbard used a dog team to get around. Now he uses a snowmobile and sometimes a helicopter or boat.

golden and white-tailed eagles, which have become rare elsewhere in Europe—have built sheltered nesting places amidst the jagged cliffs on the coast. Reindeer hooves are well adapted to navigate through the deep snows and to dig for lichen. The Norwegians learned to make flat bread from fish when there was no grain. Today they also survey and clean the bottom of the ocean near their shores with high-tech equipment to try to keep the environment safe for all to use, finding everything from shipwrecks to bottles of wine.

A Kaleidoscope of Landscapes

Because of its great length, its intricate coast, and its many mountains, valleys, and lowlands, Norway's climate and landscape vary a great deal. No one valley is ever the same two days in a row, for the sun and clouds create different lights and shadows each day amidst the different layers of rock. Much of West Norway is called "umbrella country" because of the frequent heavy rains, yet in some eastern inland valleys irrigation may be needed in dry spring weather. In the winter the snow in many areas is so deep (measured in yards, not inches), some roads are simply closed for months, while others are plowed with extra-heavy modern equipment. Miles of railroad track must be shielded with lean-tos built to keep the snow off the tracks. Some areas see 220 days of snow yearly; others 120 days and even fewer in parts of the south and southwest.

Scotch pine and Norway spruce forests grow in the north and east. Oak, ash, and beech do well in parts of the south, although a few miles away on the mountain slopes, where summer is short and winter severe, these trees cannot grow. Sheep and other animals may graze for a great part of the year near the Arctic Circle in the Lofoten Islands, while cattle must be fed inside for at least nine months in much of eastern Norway.

For Norwegians, each area has a special quality that comes from its geography and the ways people survive there—by fishing, hunting, stock rearing, growing grains or vegetables, doing forestry or manufacturing work—along with the local dialect and local folklore. Types of behavior are associated with different regions. Some areas are thought of as producing particularly musical people (Telemark) or particularly quarrelsome (Vågå in Gudbrandsdalen) or witty and critical people (Trondheim). Residents of the north are said to be more informal and open than those of the south. Part of a Norwegian's identity still comes from the place of birth or the rural origins of his or her parents or grandparents.

Because there is so little arable land, in the past farming was carried out wherever possible even though this meant many farms were self-contained and isolated, surrounded by land and forests, rather than by neighbors. Meeting places were at crossroads or at chapels rather than at village squares. Towns tended to be small. Some national statistics consider any place with more than two hundred inhabitants living close together a "town" or "urban center." By this definition, 75 percent of Norwegians live in urban settings, though only about half live in cities of ten thousand or more people. There are only three cities with populations over one hundred thousand: Oslo (457,800), Bergen (212,000), and Trondheim (137,000), with a fourth approaching this—Stavanger (98,000).

Atlantic Current

Temperatures in the inland regions, and especially in the north, can be quite cold, dropping to an icy −76°F (−60°C) in midwinter in the northeast county of Finnmark, whose coast is cooled throughout the year by the pack ice of the Barents Sea. Still, Norway is quite habitable for a land so far north. This is due to the warming effects of the Atlantic Current, a branch of the Gulf Stream, which travels along the Norwegian coast. Originating in the Caribbean Sea, waters of the Gulf Stream warmed by the hot Caribbean sun are 18–27°F (10–15°C) warmer than the surrounding ocean. Winter winds blowing from the west are also warmed by the Gulf Stream.

During the winter the western coastal strip and islands experience remarkably high temperatures. The Lofoten Islands are about 45°F (25°C) warmer than the average of other areas at this latitude. In contrast to the Baltic Sea, which freezes every winter, the Atlantic coast and most fjords remain ice free, allowing fishing boats, tankers, and now oil rigs in the Atlantic to operate in the cold but open waters. Grain crops can be cultivated on the west coast as far north as latitude 71°, whereas latitude 65° is the northernmost limit inland; and in good years (when summer frosts stay away) potatoes are grown right up to the North Cape.

Many geologists speak of the modern age as the "postglacial period," but others suggest it is more accurate to speak of our time as an interglacial period that has seen important small-scale climatic variations with brief cold periods 8,000 years ago, 5,000 years ago, 2,500 years ago, and during the last 300 years. The last "little Ice Age" brought harsh winters and cold rainy summers to Norwegian valley farming communities in 1750 and again in 1850, when there were mass emigrations to North America. By 1950 the climate had improved again, and the little Ice Age seems to have come to an end.

Light and Darkness

Norway's location so far north creates a very special annual rhythm of light and darkness that affects animal life, vegetation, and the attitudes and social lives of the Norwegians themselves. Because of the tilt of the earth as it travels around the sun, the North Pole is tilted away from the sun in the winter and toward the sun in the summer. North of the Arctic Circle the sun is not visible for weeks in the winter, just as it never sets in the summer. To combat the darkness of the long winter, Norwegians consume the greatest amount of electricity per person in the world. The appearance of the bright northern lights in the northern skies is greeted with excitement as they shatter the darkness with high-energy fireworks of color.

Norway's northern latitude means there is a special intensity to the light, different from that in lower latitudes. The mingling of moonlight, starlight, and light reflected from snow creates an unusual effect. And because the sun drops below the horizon at a shallow angle, dawn and dusk last for long periods before and after the sun is visible.

Land of the Midnight Sun

In the summer the sun remains above the horizon for the same length of time that it is absent in the winter. The large area from North Cape to the Arctic Circle is called "the land of the midnight sun" and attracts visitors by the thousands. As one goes south, the length of time

When the sun reappears in late January, after two months of continual darkness, children in Tromsø get the day off from school to watch its arrival. They have to be prompt to greet the sun, for on that first day it is above the horizon only four minutes. Ola Røe

North Cape

North Cape is a sheer rocky cliff that plunges vertically 1,000 ft. (300 m.) into the icy waves of the Arctic Ocean. At north latitude 71°10'21" it is the northernmost point of western Europe, except for a flat tongue of land nearby that extends about 5,000 ft. (1,500 m.) farther. Standing at its edge, one feels at the end of the world. Below is an ice-cold ocean that seems to stretch toward infinity. Somewhere over the horizon lies the immense and forbidding snow of the North Pole.

The first person to record this feeling was Francesco Negri, an Italian cleric who in the seventeenth century set out from his native Ravenna determined to see the northernmost part of Europe. He learned to ski in Sweden and journeyed up the coast of Norway by horseback and by boat. He traveled alone: "How was I to find a fellow traveler with a body of iron and courage forged in bronze?" He told no one he was a Catholic priest and traveled in winter, the most difficult season. He bundled up against the cold, wearing two pairs of mittens and a fur hat that covered his face and neck so completely that he could barely breathe. When he reached his destination in 1664, he wrote in his journal:

"Here I am at the North Cape, in the remotest part of Finnmark, and I may just as well describe it as the remotest part of the earth, since there is no place further north that is inhabited by man-kind, my thirst for knowledge has been satisfied. . . ."

North Cape is on the small island of Magerøy, "Meager Island," a ferry's ride from the mainland. The eastern part consists of a wild, rugged group of mountains; toward the west and northwest is a wide plateau; in the middle of the island are many small peaks and little lakes. No trees grow here. On the exposed and weather-beaten topsoil only the hardiest plants can survive. In the summertime reindeer find food in the grass and moss.

The Sami people, who lived in the far north long before Norwegians came as permanent settlers, had a place of sacrifice near the creek of Hornvika, and there are other holy Sami sites on the island as well.

A few animals—hare, otter, and mink—find their way to the island. Away from the windblown mountaintops, there are occasionally some flowers near sheltered creeks. Picking them is strictly forbidden. Plant and animal life on Magerøy have been protected by law since 1929.

People live year round in several small fishing villages and harbors, such as Skarsvåg on the east coast, the world's most northerly fishing hamlet, and Honningsvåg, the main port, where more than 5,000 ships call each year.

From ancient times the towering precipice of North Cape has been an important landmark. Sailors knew they had to sail north up the coast till the North Cape and then turn east or west. Ola Røe

The Midnight Sun

Because the earth's axis of rotation is tilted, the length of day and night varies from one place to another and according to the season of the year. At the equator, there is hardly any noticeable difference between summer and winter, and day and night last for twelve hours each at all times of the year. The seasonal variations become greater as one goes toward the poles.

The farther north one goes in Norway, the longer there is a period of continuous daylight. In the summer, the midnight sun lasts:

in Tromsø	from May 20 to July 23
in Hammerfest	from May 16 to July 27
at the North Cape	from May 14 to July 29
on Svalbard	from April 21 to August 22

the sun does not set declines, but in all places north of the Arctic Circle, the sun never sets on Midsummer Day (June 23), which has been celebrated since pagan times with bonfires and special gatherings.

Even in the south of Norway summer nights are bright, with only a few hours of twilight. People can read newspapers at midnight by natural light. They walk their dogs or meet friends at two in the morning. Norwegians say they have two days every day in the summer: one for working (which with flexible hours could be from 7 A.M. to 2 P.M. or from 8 A.M. to 3 P.M.) and one for *hverdagslivet* ("everyday life").

When plant life awakens from the dark winter, flowers and berries explode with intensity. In central and eastern Norway crops are grown for fodder for cows, goats, and sheep. Though the number of days for growing are limited, because of the length of the long summer days the actual ripening time is almost comparable to that of the southern Mediterranean, since plants can grow during the night. In many areas, sheep and goats are still taken to the mountains to graze in the summer, though the tradition of the farmer's wife, children, and cows moving to a *seter* (mountain hut) is no longer followed. Nowadays the mountain huts have often become summer cottages for urban relatives. In the north reindeer may start their summer with an icy swim to an island where they can roam freely for summer pasturing.

Rhythms of the Sea

Three quarters of all Norwegians live within ten miles of the sea. It is said that "a Norwegian is never happy too far away from the smell of fish." Many Norwegians have turned to the sea and followed the annual rhythms of the cod, herring, and other fish. In the past, Norwegians spoke of the sea uniting and the land dividing, and until recently it was easier to leave Norway's west coast and sail for the British Isles than to cross the mountains to the southeast. In the last few decades, coastal communities have been linked through new tunnels, bridges, roads, and much-used airplanes, but there are still important water routes too. Every day, for a hundred years, the *hurtigruta*, (literally "fast route") or coastal express, has passed along the west coast carrying cargo and passengers to communities far from other modes of transportation. Cars cannot drive directly from Stavanger to Bergen, but there are fast hydrofoils and catamarans. Other ferries link farms and small villages along the fjords.

Surrounded by water to the north, west, and south, Norwegians have age-old traditions of seafaring, whether as adventurers or colonists, fishers or whalers, or more recently as sailors of merchant ships and luxury liners. Since 1875 Norway has been one of the great maritime nations. In the past it was often wiser to set off for distant shores than to divide the family's small homestead, particularly along the coasts, where small farms huddled in between mountains and sea and there was no room to expand.

In the mid-1960's the Norwegian government allowed testing for oil in the rough North Sea. Just as fish catches were declining from overfishing and ecological imbalances, the sea gave Norway another source of income and employment. This has created an extraordinary new chapter in Norwegian economy and politics.

Over time Norwegians have fished their seas, rivers, and lakes, mined the earth, and farmed every inch of land possible. They have come to realize that though they have overcome many obstacles, the environment of the north is an especially vulnerable one. By the early 1970's the delicate balance was very shaky. Overfishing through the use of elaborate nets, vacuums, and fishing factories, along with the impact of foreign trawlers, depleted the supply of fish. There are serious pollution problems from Norway's own factories and agricultural fertilizers and even more from Great Britain, continental Europe, and the former Soviet republics. Drilling for oil has greatly helped the balance of payments, but there is still a broader issue for the future: how to balance social and economic interests with the fragile environment of the north. This is a dilemma the Norwegians know they must solve.

The People of Norway

From the perspective of global history, Norway has been settled only recently. Until some 13,000 years ago this large northern stretch of land at the top of Europe was covered with ice. Gradually, over at least 3,000 years, small parts of the coast and eventually the whole area resurfaced.

About 9,000 years ago most of the country that is today's Norway was finally free of ice and habitable by animals and human beings. Some areas, such as the southern highlands, were not occupied for another 2,000 years, because it took a long while for a plant cover to grow, which then attracted grazing reindeer and later groups of hunters.

Archaeologists do not have a complete picture of the exact routes or dates of the first migrations into Norway. There is evidence of early habitation along the northern coast of Finnmark (called Komsa culture), as well as along the west coast and on the mountain plateau on the east side of the Oslo Fjord (called Fosna culture). Bands of hunters lived and fished close to the shore and hunted big game, notably reindeer and elk, inland. Ecological conditions were stable, and the yield from hunting wild reindeer and fishing was almost inexhaustible.

The most northern finds (dating from 7,000 or 8,000 B.C. to 1,000 or 2,000 B.C.) are especially intriguing to archaeologists because they were so far away from other settlements (except for the similar finds on the Kola Peninsula in the Russian Republic) and it is unclear how people got there. Some theorists believe there was migration through eastern Finland and Russia, while others propose a route from the southwest up the west coast of Norway.

Whatever picture eventually emerges, we can be sure that in the early settlement of Norway, there were migrations from east and south of peoples who were ancestors of both the Sami and Norwegians of today. Only a few skeletal remains of the early residents are available, but they indicate several populations with differences in bone structure and other physical characteristics.

Culture Contact and Change

While the earliest inhabitants survived by hunting and gathering, by 5,000 years ago some people were farming and raising cattle, with varying degrees of success. Many types of prehistoric pottery, tools, burial practices, rock carvings, and trade goods are similar to those found in Denmark and Sweden.

Archaeological finds dating from the first to the fourth centuries A.D. include large bronze bowls and buckets of a type unknown in Denmark and Sweden. They are evidence of direct trade with Celtic people across the North Sea to western Norway. Some harbors on the southwest coast of Norway must have served as ports, such as the district

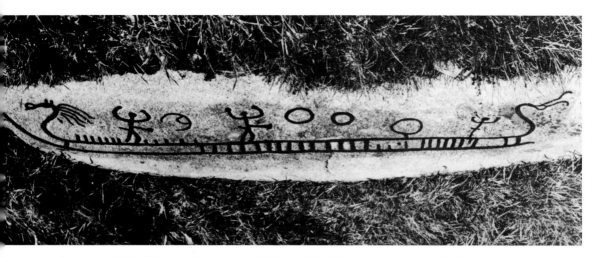

Carvings chiseled into rocks between 4,000 and 9,000 years ago are found through-out Norway on mountainsides, near rivers, and in fields. Northern Europe's largest rock carvings are found in Alta in Finnmark and probably date back 6,500 years. Some carvings represent animals that were hunted. Later ones reflect agricultural scenes and boats, such as this longboat and crew in Østfold. Norwegian Information Service, New York

around the present-day town of Haugesund, which has yielded particularly rich graves. One contains more gold than has been found in any other burial in northern Europe from this time period. Thus, even before the Vikings, Norwegians on the west coast were making boats and establishing trading connections across the North Sea.

Similarities and Differences

Norway is a sparsely populated country whose population is spread unevenly throughout the land. Some areas are literally empty regions where bare mountains prevent the smallest flowers from growing. By international standards Norway has a small and homogeneous population. Only about 3 percent are foreign born. Norway has two indigenous ethnic minorities: Norwegian Finns and Sami.

Norwegians share many common culture traits. These include a Lutheran heritage with a strong missionary tradition and a concern for

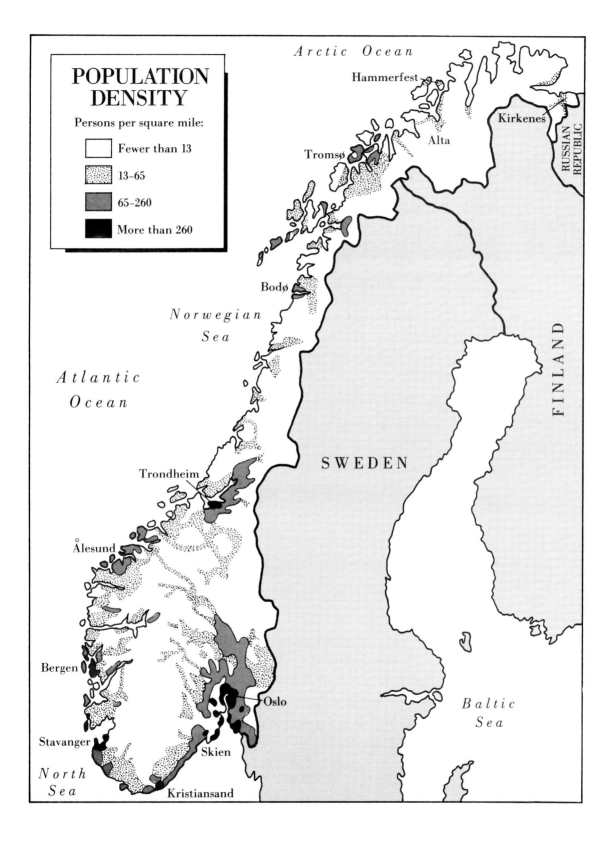

POPULATION
DENSITY

Persons per square mile:

Fewer than 13

13–65

65–260

More than 260

Arctic Ocean

Hammerfest

Kirkenes

Alta

Tromsø

RUSSIAN REPUBLIC

Norwegian Sea

Bodø

Atlantic Ocean

FINLAND

SWEDEN

Trondheim

Ålesund

Bergen

Oslo

Stavanger

Skien

Baltic Sea

North Sea

Kristiansand

The benches on Karl Johansgate, the main pedestrian shopping street in the center of Oslo, become popular as the sun comes out in March.   Peter Udbjørg

human rights, an interest in the world beyond, a respect for the rule of law, and a stress on individual self-reliance. In a recent survey of what is associated with "Norwegianness," most people mentioned the humorous folktale "The Woman Against the Stream" by Peter Christian Asbjørnsen (1812–1885) and Jørgen Moe (1813–1882), which depicts a stubborn, independent woman who follows her own ideas, no matter what the cost.

Norwegians are fond of finding "Norwegian" traits in folk or fairy tales and in various noted Norwegian writers, but are quick to argue about particular customs, such as what the proper Norwegian Christmas menu should be—an issue complicated by different regional traditions. They all agree that the Norwegian flag should be displayed often and that Norway is both a very old and a very young nation.

Norwegians call themselves Scandinavians or people of Norden (the North), though the term Nordic is also used. Norwegians agree that they are not all as tall, blond, and blue eyed as the tourist posters project, but reflect a mixing of groups with Germanic and Celtic heritage as well as occasional shipwrecked southern Europeans. A person from the west coast may have black hair and dark-blue eyes; one from the southeastern valleys ash-blond hair and light-blue eyes.

Differences among regions and Norwegian dialects are often stressed. One joke goes: "All Norwegians speak four languages, but three of them are Norwegian." This refers to the disagreement about what form the national language should take. Modern Norwegian speakers are divided between two different official Norwegian languages: Bokmål and Nynorsk.

The Languages of Norway

The Sami language is not a Germanic language, as Norwegian is. It is part of the Finno-Ugric language family, related to Finnish and Hungarian. Sami speakers are divided into six different dialectical groups and on occasion must speak Norwegian to understand each other, although North Sami is becoming the standard form. Many Sami are bi- or trilingual.

Norwegian and English are related languages, since they both evolved from a common North Germanic. English, German, Dutch, and Frisian split off long ago, leaving Common Scandinavian, which was spoken from about A.D. 550 to 1050. This Common Scandinavian was the parent language for six official, literary languages in Scandinavia, plus a great variety of spoken dialects.

These modern languages, in the vocabulary of linguists, are Danish, Dano-Norwegian and New Norwegian (both spoken in Norway), Swedish, Faeroese (spoken in the Faeroe Islands), and Icelandic. The oldest written examples of any Germanic language are the runic inscriptions in Scandinavia.

By A.D. 900 there were some distinctions between Old Western Scandinavian, sometimes called Old Norse (parent language of Norwegian, Faeroese and Icelandic), and Old Eastern Scandinavian (parent language of Danish and Swedish), though the differences were smaller than they are today. Norwegian became a written language in the early twelfth century.

Because of the political strength of Denmark, Danish had a strong influence on the Norwegian language. From the 1500's to 1814 Danish was the official written language in Norway. From 1814 to 1905, while Norway was in a union with Sweden, Danish still continued to be the language of public administration. This form was referred to as "Riksmål" (literally, the language of the realm). Norwegians spoke their own local dialect at home. However, a growing national movement

Along the coasts, especially in the south, Norwegians take to boats on Midsummer's Eve, and the waters get particularly crowded.   The Royal Norwegian Ministry of Foreign Affairs, Oslo

Norwegian for the Twentieth Century:
Bokmål vs. Nynorsk

There have been two different approaches to creating a modern Norwegian language since the mid-nineteenth century.

1. One model (Landsmål, "language of the countryside," later named Nynorsk, New Norwegian) sought to build a new Norwegian language as close as possible to what Norwegian might have been had it continued without Danish domination. Ivar Aasen (1813–1896), a linguist and poet, analyzed western dialects and formulated the written norm for Nynorsk in *Norsk Grammatik* (*Norwegian Grammar*) (1864) and *Norse Ordbog* (*Norwegian Dictionary*) (1873).

Since he drew on rural dialects, Nynorsk has great strength in poetic and literary terms describing nature and personal matters. Nynorsk is not the "native" language of any Norwegian speakers, and it never became the first language of Norway; but it has long had a group of supporters who associate it with a more democratic national consciousness and see Bokmål as a form of Danish.

2. The other model (Riksmål, "language of the realm," later named Bokmål, "book language") used Danish as the base and "Norwegianized" it through changes in vocabulary, spelling, and pronunciation. It built on the speech and writings of the educated urban population. In 1856 Knud Knudsen (1812–1895), a linguist and edu-

in the mid-nineteenth century reopened the question of what the standard Norwegian language should be. Some preferred a new, less Danish language, which they called Landsmål (now called Nynorsk or New Norwegian).

cator, advocated a step-by-step Norwegianization of Danish spelling—
a policy followed by such leading writers of the time as Bjørnstjerne
Bjørnson (1832–1910) and Henrik Ibsen (1828–1906). Over the years
Bokmål has retained much of the Danish vocabulary while accepting
some of the Nynorsk sound system.

Failed Compromise   After spelling reforms in 1907, 1917,
1938, and 1959, which were intended to make the two languages
closer, some Norwegians hoped for a merger of the two languages into
"Samnorsk" (United Norwegian). Students reacted in 1960 by burning
books translated into Samnorsk and had banners reading *"Samnorsk
er ikke norsk"* ("Samnorsk is not Norwegian"). In spite of many parliamentary committees and studies, Samnorsk was never accepted. Today
Bokmål and Nynorsk exist side by side.

Since 1925 all government officials have been required to answer
letters in the language in which they are written, which means that all
bureaucrats must be competent in both forms, and in fact so must all
high school graduates. Local school boards decide which form will be
used in elementary school, and the current split is about 20 percent
Nynorsk and 80 percent Bokmål. Most newspapers are published in
Bokmål, though the minority has its own theater and is still quite vo-
cal, especially when the language question gets combined with other
national policy questions such as membership in the European
Community (EC), which the Nynorsk adherents generally oppose.

The language question has been a political and emotional issue for
at least 150 years. In 1910 a prime minister (whose party supported
Riksmål) was removed from office because he made some vaguely sup-
portive comments about the language of the rural people during a fes-

tive occasion. Regardless of which written form they use, all Norwegian speakers can understand each other.

Norwegian Finns

Finns (called Kvener in Norwegian) were involved in trade in the north as far back as the twelfth century. From the early eighteenth century through the nineteenth century, a number came from northern Finland, looking for a more secure life in the Norwegian fjords of Troms and Finnmark. Some were pushed by marauding Russians who crossed the border between Russia and Sweden-Finland. Others fled the Russo-Swedish wars and then the famine years of the 1860's. Vadsø, at the far eastern coast of Norway, called "Vesi-saari" (water island in Finnish), became the best-known Kven center. At one time the Finnish settlers were in the majority: In 1875, 62 percent of the population at Vadsø was Finnish-speaking, but very little Finnish is heard today.

In the twentieth century Finns have moved to Sweden more than to Norway, but there are still about 12,000 Finnish speakers in Norway; they are mostly bilingual and contribute to the cultural pluralism of the north. The Sami library in Karasjok has two alternating bookmobile routes: One week books go out in Norwegian and Sami, the next week in Finnish and Sami.

The Sami People

The Sami are an indigenous people who have lived throughout all four countries of Fennoscandia (Norway, Sweden, Finland, and the Kola Peninsula of the Russian Republic) for thousands of years. About two thirds of all modern Sami, or about 30,000 people, are estimated to live in Norway. The Sami are enjoying a revival of interest in their language and culture and have been empowered through the Sami Parliament, opened in October 1989, to speak as a group on the many issues concerning their place in Norway.

In Old Norse the Sami were called Finner (Finders), indicating they were people who could locate game and find their way in wild country. The northern county of Finnmark, which means "Sami borderland," is where more than half of the Norwegian Sami live today.

The name Lapp appeared later and was used in particular in Finland, Sweden, and Russia. The people themselves prefer the name that appears as Same in Norwegian, Sami in English, and Saemie, Saapmie, Sapme, Sabmi, Saam, or Saami in their various dialects.

Like Native Americans, the Sami are eager for outsiders to see beyond the stereotypes based on early travelers' accounts and museum displays. However, some of the early images and traditional patterns of behavior, which surprised outsiders, reflect Sami strengths and have become powerful symbols of Sami identity.

Early commentators, such as the Roman historian Tacitus in A.D. 98, were surprised that the Sami dressed in animal skins and traveled quickly on narrow pieces of wood (the earliest skis), and that Sami women hunted alongside men. These hunters adapted well to their environment and used their catches to provide not only meat, blood sausage, and clothing, but also sinew thread, skin-covered cradles, and bone-marrow pacifiers for their babies.

During the fifteenth century Norwegians began to invade the Sami area, which extended across the north and halfway down the Atlantic coast, depleting the stocks of wild game. Some Sami responded by becoming full-time reindeer breeders and herders, organized in cooperative groups called *siida*, based on kin ties. They frequently crossed international borders (established only in 1752 and 1826) in the mountainous tundra and became known as mountain Sami. Others on the coast and the fjords, coastal Sami, continued their old patterns of hunting and fishing, adding boat making for themselves and Norwegian settlers.

Starting in the mid-1700's, each summer Russians from the White Sea area brought flour, timber, hemp, and other important goods, which they exchanged for fish. This form of barter was advantageous for the Sami. In summer, when the fish were often infested with worms, the Russians were the only ones who bought them. This trade was known as the Pomor Trade, based on the Russian words *po* meaning "by," and *more,* meaning "sea." The trading stopped in 1917, when the borders closed after the Russian Revolution.

Reindeer Herding

Paulus Utsi (1918–1975) and Inger Huuva-Utsi (1914–1984), Sami poets and reindeer drivers, referred to the nomadic life of the Sami, and to the pressures to conform to mainstream standards, when they wrote:

> *Our life*
> *is like a ski track*
> *on the white plateau*
> *which the wind erases*
> *before the day breaks.*

Translated by Harald Gaski

Though the wind may erase the track, the life of reindeer nomads has long had a regular annual pattern: a long stay at a winter base in the forests where herds feed on lichen under the snow and on trees, a spring migration toward the coast with a pause for calving, then a short trip to summer grazing areas on peninsulas and islands. Coastal residents in Finnmark say that the surest sign of spring is the sight of a

Today only about 7 percent of Sami are reindeer pastoralists (herders and breeders). Still, reindeer and the mobility associated with the annual herding cycle are important aspects of Sami identity. There are more than twenty different terms for reindeer in the Sami language—based on age, sex, size, color of hair, shape of horns, and even type of cry—showing how important the reindeer are to the Sami. Ola Røe

Some Sami still spend part of the year in a traditional lavvo *(skin tent). A lavvo was put up in front of the Storting to protest the Alta dam project, and the new Sami parliament building is similarly shaped.*   Ola Røe

colorfully dressed nomad skiing over the hill. The autumn migration back to camp includes a reindeer roundup, in which some are slaughtered and the young calves are given their identifying ear marks.

Obstacles to Reindeer Herding   Reindeer pasturage and migration routes, all on public lands, are more and more seriously disturbed by dams, roads, national parks, sports fishing and hunting, tourism, mining, and military bases. Pollution is another serious threat. The Chernobyl nuclear explosion in 1986 especially affected the 2000 south Sami living in Mid Norway, who were forced to slaughter their herds due to the high level of radioactivity.

A major test of Sami rights was the Alta-Kautokeino River hydroelectric project proposed in 1970. Sami, environmentalists, and advo-

· 32 ·

cates for ethnic rights mobilized against the dam, which would interfere with migratory routes of the Sami. Despite a level of activism unusual in Norway, including sit-ins and arrests in the largest police action since World War II, the project was approved by Norway's parliament, the Storting ("stor" meaning large and "ting" meaning assembly), and the Supreme Court in 1982. The Alta protests gave a strong push to Sami consciousness and political organizing.

Sami/State Relations

Only two thirds of the Sami speak any of the Sami dialects, since there were strong attempts by missionaries, agricultural experts, and schoolteachers from the 1850's to the 1950's to "Norwegianize" the Sami.

Sami Revivalism

Some Sami fought attempts at Norwegianization. In the 1850's they reacted to negative Norwegian attitudes toward their language and customs by rejecting the Norwegians in return, often through involvement in a Christian revival movement called Laestadianism. Started by Lars Levi Laestadius (1800–1861), a Swedish Lutheran minister who was part Sami, the reform movement made over 20,000 converts in Sweden, Finland, and Norway—of whom at least half were Sami.

The Laestadians defined Norwegian language, dress, and schooling as profane and sinful, while Sami poverty was defined as sacred. Speaking in tongues, dancing, and trances were accepted parts of the religious ecstasy, though older Sami shamanistic trances had been outlawed. Laestadianism continues to play an important role in North Norway as a movement within the Evangelical Lutheran State Church.

The Joik *Tradition*

The *joik*, a type of yodeling, is an old Sami form of musical expression. Some *joik*s imitate animals—the wolf, the wild or domestic reindeer, the long-tailed duck. Others tell ancient myths or the history of the Sami or make social commentary about events or individuals.

The most popular *joik*s today are character sketches about people. They can be changed as the person changes. No one writes his or her own *joik*, but once one is written about a person, it is said that the *joik* "belongs" to that person. The memory of a deceased person may be kept alive through his or her *joik*s.

In older religious ceremonies the *joik* was used to help the shaman go into a trance while playing a drum. During the Norwegianization process, *joik*s and drumming were made illegal. Today *joik*ing has acquired a new value as a cultural symbol. Recently one was at the top of the Norwegian hit parade.

In the 1960's the official position of the government began to shift from a policy of Norwegianization to a policy of accommodation and even support. Research projects focusing on Sami language and culture have produced new curricula for all levels of the educational system. Today students may choose Sami as their first language in some communities.

The Sami themselves have become involved in Sami newspapers, a radio station, and a major research library housed in Karasjok. New museums have opened, and new Sami theater groups have been formed.

The Sami film *Veiviseren* (*The Pathfinder*) by the young Sami filmmaker Nils Gaup, based on an old Sami legend about invading outsiders, was nominated for an American Academy Award for best for-eign-language feature in 1988.

In early 1988 the Norwegian constitution was changed. The Storting added to the constitution Article 110A, which states: "It is the responsi-bility of the authorities of the State to create conditions enabling the Sami people to preserve and develop their language, culture, and way of life." Sami went to the polls throughout Norway in September 1989 to elect their own thirty-nine-person parliament, housed in Karasjok; this body draws up recommendations on all Sami issues for the Storting. Optimists hope that these new channels of communication will be more than ceremonial; pessimists fear that the basic issues of Sami rights to land and water have not been resolved.

The West

At the dawn of Norway's prehistory people moved onto the west coast, probably up from around Denmark. Based on the remains of bones in early cave sites, archaeologists describe the coastal area as one of unbounded natural wealth, with great schools of whales and seals as well as fish of great variety and supply. Sea fowl on islands provided eggs and down, while wild animals, including red deer and reindeer, roamed the woods. Bones of fifty different animals were found in one cave, including bears, who must have come to the shore to catch fish. Fishhooks, arrowheads, spears, harpoons for catching seals, sewing needles, scrapers used in cleaning hides—all of good design and remarkable efficiency—have been found, as well as rock tracings of land animals and whales. Early tools of bone and horn were gradually replaced by stone axes of flint and quartz and later bronze, through trade with central and southern Europe.

Fishing was later supplemented with simple farming on the sparse island and coastal lands or inland along fjords. Beyond the protected coastal waters the open sea not only provided a livelihood but was for a long time the major route to the outside world: for trade with the Roman Empire, for expeditions of the Vikings, for colonists, explorers, and merchant fleets. As early as A.D. 874 dried cod was exported to England for Lent; there it was traded for grain, honey, and cloth. The mystery of how the fish got to England was solved only in 1980, when Danish archaeologists were able to raise up four sunken Viking ships and found that one had a different shape suitable for carrying cargo—most Viking ships were built for carrying just a crew—and that it was from Norway.

What Norwegians today call Vestlandet ("the West" or "the West Country") comprises the islands and the coastal areas up to Mid Norway, including the major port cities of Bergen and Stavanger and the fishing towns of Haugesund ("the town built on herring bones"), Ålesund, and Kristiansund; and also inland areas.

The inland areas contain small farms and electro-metallurgical industry along the fjords. Agricultural lowlands in Jaeren, south of Stavanger, supply about half of Norway's agricultural produce, milk, and some of its Jarlsberg cheese. Further inland there is an area where up to 200,000 sheep and goats move uplands into the Sirdal Mountains every spring and summer and then back to the valleys, partway by truck, in the fall.

The West's fjord districts include what are probably the world's most northerly fruit-growing districts, where the mountain walls have an oven effect, holding in the sun's heat and allowing apples, pears, and plums to grow on the steep slopes. Mountains, glaciers, and sparsely settled highlands divide the West from the East.

The West Country is the Norway that is best known to the rest of the world—the Norway of the steamer that goes to the North Cape; the

Norway of beautiful and well-kept villages and coastal towns nestled into a backdrop of majestic mountains. The ancestors of many Norwegian Americans left from this area in the nineteenth century. The West is also fjord country, where company towns, built near hydro-electric stations and deep sheltered waterways, have replaced quaint isolated farms. The towns haven't ruined the fjords. The visitor sees the fjord as awe-inspiring, but, especially in the past, the reality of living every day isolated from the next fjord by huge, gray, towering mountains has also been described as overwhelming, frightening, and depressingly difficult.

Fjords are like sunken valleys, filled by the ocean cutting through high hills or mountains. To travel on a "fjord bus" boat or cruise liner between steep mountains to the end of an inlet is a spectacular experience and one that is forever different, since no two fjords are alike. Norwegian Tourist Board, New York

The busy fishing port of Ålesund is built on several islands. Ålesund means "eel's sound." The water wiggles between the islands like an eel, though some say this fish-processing center looks like a fishhook out into the Atlantic. Sunnmørsposten (Ålesund's local newspaper)

Blue Meadow

Most of Vestlandet's history and identity are associated with the sea, which the Norwegians have often called their "blue meadow." The sea has made possible fishing, shipping, and, now, fish-farming and oil exploration. Traditionally fishers from the West and North Norway supplemented their fish catch with a modest amount of whaling and hunting of harp seal and hooded seal for pelts, using their regular fishing vessels. Though there are many kinds of fish to be caught along the west coast, including capelin, haddock, saithe, and mackerel, two large midwinter fisheries stand out for their size and social impact: the Lofoten cod fishery (see North Norway in Chapter V) and the herring fisheries around Haugesund.

LAND AND PETROLEUM

MILES
0   100   200

KILOMETERS
0   100   200   300

● OIL FIELDS
○ GAS FIELDS
--- PIPELINES

Arctic
Ocean

NORTH
CAPE

RUS. REP.

LOFOTEN

FINLAND

Norwegian
Sea

SWEDEN

Atlantic
Ocean

DOVRE
MTS.

ØSTERDALEN
TRYSIL RIVER

JOTUNHEIMEN
MTS.

Highest Mountain: GALDHØPIGGEN
Largest Valley: GUDBRANDSDALEN
Largest Glacier: JOSTEDALSBREEN
Longest Fjord: SOGNE FJORD
Largest Lake: MJØSA
Longest River: GLOMMA

HALLINGDAL

Oslo

HARDANGER
PLATEAU

NUMEDAL

OSLO FJORD

SIRDAL
MTS.

Skagerrak

CONTINENTAL SHELF

North Sea

Baltic
Sea

DENMARK

In the late nineteenth century 50 percent of Stavanger's working population was involved directly or indirectly with canning, including the production of expensive lacquered paper labels, now treasured as collectors' items.   Stavanger Museum

Herring: Silver of the Sea

For years, herring returned from the open seas in large schools each winter to spawn along the coast. This migration supported not only fishing but shipbuilding, barrel and tackle making, and herring salting houses. As early as the twelfth century Pope Alexander III (1159–1181) issued an exemption from the general prohibition on Sunday fishing to allow herring to be caught. In 1273 the new national laws stated that any lawsuit should be postponed until after the herring season.

Herring has been preserved and prepared many different ways, but during the Nazi occupation (1940–1945) Norwegians largely survived on herring, eaten morning, noon, and night, dried, smoked, pickled,

Norway as a Shipping Nation

Despite Norway's long maritime traditions, international shipping on a large scale began to develop only in the mid-nineteenth century. At first the Norwegians used tall sailing ships. Between 1850 and 1875 the number of Norwegian merchant marines rose from 15,000 to 60,000, and the size of the fleet increased fivefold. The Norwegian merchant fleet was soon the third largest in the world, and it has remained in the top five ever since.

While much of the early fleet was owned by urban shipowners with a lot of money to invest, Norway also developed its sailing fleet through cooperative ownership. One could become a part owner by helping to build the ship, delivering lumber, or otherwise sharing in the enterprise. In this way a ship could be jointly owned by an entire small town or village, and an individual could be a cooperative shareholder while still farming and/or fishing. Profits from shipping contributed to the rising living standard of Norway's port populations in the second half of the nineteenth century.

fried, boiled, and marinated. Had the herring been out of cycle during the war, it is hard to imagine how the Norwegians would have survived.

Herring does come in cycles, which are not completely understood, appearing every winter for years and then disappearing for twenty or thirty years, only to return again. When herring disappeared in 1870, the residents were challenged to find new activities rather than return to the old subsistence economy. Haugesund, which had been a small town in 1870, became a major shipbuilding and shipping port, and the rocky Jaeren district south of Stavanger was cleared into agricultural lands through backbreaking work using crowbars and pulleys.

Norwegian shippers stress constant modernization and specialization. During the 1970's they helped pioneer container transportation by packing goods in special modules. Norwegian design is evident in state-of-the-art cruise vessels and high-speed catamarans that have replaced older ferries in Norway and around the world.

Today Norway has over two hundred shipping companies, many family owned, with a wide range of types of vessels and scale of operations. About 90 percent of the fleet sails between various foreign ports without ever touching Norway. Norwegian schools sometimes "adopt" ships as class projects and send letters and gifts to the crew while they are at sea. The sailors in return send souvenirs from their ports of call back to the classrooms for study and visit "their" schools when they return to port. The percentage of Norwegian sailors on Norwegian-owned ships has declined in recent years due to the rise in wages Norwegians expect, but the officers are still usually Norwegian.

Stavanger, which had exported 200,000 barrels of herring a year during the peak years, turned to canning and became the center for canned sardines.

Bergen: Window to the West

Haugesund and Stavanger are newer cities compared to Bergen, which stood out as the "window to the west" even before its official founding by King Olav III, "the Peaceful," (reigned 1069–1093) in 1070. Unlike Norway's other major cities, Trondheim and Oslo, which are each surrounded by fertile farming districts, Bergen has no fertile lands and lies amidst seven mountains facing the sea. Said to have been a starting point for some Viking expeditions, Bergen grew as a fishing and trading port. In the thirteenth century special agreements were made with German towns to trade fish and furs for grains. The Hanseatic League—a *hansa* (association) of north German seaport trading towns—opened its counting houses at Bryggen, the part of the city overlooking the harbor. Bergen prospered while the rest of Norway suffered from a variety of ills. Even after the power of the League was broken in the sixteenth century Bergen continued to monopolize the fish trade of the whole coast and for a while surpassed Copenhagen, Denmark, in importance as a great trading port. After 1803 northern fishers could sell their catch in Bodø close to home, but most preferred the difficult trip to Bergen because it was an adventure.

"I am not from Norway, I am from Bergen!"

Bergen has always been a cosmopolitan town, in many ways set apart from the Norwegian countryside. German, Dutch, Scottish, and Danish merchants dominated the commercial life of the city, giving it an international atmosphere. Even in the 1990's people from Bergen are known for their extreme local pride, as expressed in the standard joke: "I am not from Norway, I am from Bergen!"

In 1814, when the Norwegian constitution was written, only 10 percent of Norway's population of 900,000 lived in towns, with 18,000 inhabitants in Bergen and about 10,000 people in the capital, Christiania (now Oslo). Bergen's merchants spent their money on beautiful country estates, but they also invested in parks, music, and theater. The first known theatrical performance in Norway was given at the Cathedral

School under the auspices of the humanist Absalon Pedersson Beyer (1528–1575), whose principal work, *Om Norigs Rige (Concerning the Kingdom of Norway)*, was written in 1567. Bergen has the oldest orchestra in the country, was the home of the composer Edvard Grieg (1843–1907), and currently hosts an annual international music festival.

Today Bergen is the second largest city of Norway (population 212,000) and is still the principal port on the west coast, with a considerable merchant fleet and several large shipyards and one of Norway's four universities. Many fish processing and canning plants have moved to northern Norway to be nearer the fishing grounds, and the extensive use of airlines, railroads, and automobiles in recent years has diminished some of the importance of Bergen's coastal location. New firms may be more likely to choose to locate in Oslo, the nation's capital, or in Stavanger, the "oil capital," but Bergen is also important in the new "petroleum era" and has great dignity associated with its history as the most cosmopolitan of Norwegian cities.

The Norwegian "Bible Belt"

There has always been some tension between the city and the countryside in the West, expressed in discussions of dialects and of religion. In the late eighteenth century cities, especially Bergen, were seen as un-Norwegian and as tied to commercial values rather than "Christian" ideals. In the 1790's a pietist movement, led by Hans Nielsen Hauge (1771–1824), arose, stressing an ethic of hard work and personal salvation. Though Hauge spent ten years in jail for preaching without a license, the movement was eventually incorporated into the State Lutheran Church as the Indremisjon (the Inner Mission).

The Indremisjon has its own rural prayer houses and lay preachers, often retired farmers. Since 1907 it has also had its own theological school. Believers have a strict moral code: no drinking or dancing are allowed, and a commitment to charity and drug-free lives is stressed. Most members of the Inner Mission are rural, older, poorer, and less educated than nonmembers.

Their influence is larger than their numbers. Alexander Kielland (1849–1906), one-time mayor of Stavanger and noted novelist, was prevented from receiving a state stipend because of objections from the pietists. As late as the 1950's there was a dispute over the interpretation of "eternal damnation" that went to the Storting. Norwegians refer to a "Bible Belt" today extending from Kristiansand in the south through the southwest and up to Ålesund.

Social historians wonder about the causes of this movement on the west coast. Did life involve more of a struggle against nature here, against the sea and the rocky soil? Was the contrast with the cosmopolitan centers of Bergen and later Stavanger significant? Was there more potential for a community prayer house in the West, where there was less economic difference between farmers than in East Norway, where small and large farmers felt estranged from each other? Whatever the reasons, for two hundred years the pietist movement has been strong in the West.

One recent change, which may reflect some decline in religious views, was the introduction of Sunday newspapers in January 1991; until then they had been illegal throughout Norway, partially due to the influence of the pietists.

Black Gold

During hearings in Geneva in 1958, when Norway sought to extend its territorial waters, geologists testified that one could disregard the possibility of finding oil, gas, or sulphur in the continental shelf along the Norwegian coast, since Norway's shelf was too old and there was no oil on land. But after gas was discovered in Holland in 1962, two representatives from Phillips Petroleum in Oklahoma approached Trygve Lie (1896–1968), former Secretary General of the United Nations (1946–1953), about the possibility of exploring for oil off Norway. He replied, "I believe you must have made a mistake . . . Norway has no oil or gas."

Nine years later oil was flowing. Seventeen oil companies drilled the seabed of the North Sea to find this much-fought-over resource. Norwegian companies contributed survey vessels with complex sonar equipment and computer instruments to make detailed marine seismic surveys. Shipping companies designed and built a fleet of gigantic semisubmersible rigs, jack-ups (drilling platforms that stand on the

Norwegian oil production is small compared with that of Saudi Arabia but is still growing. The Norwegian shelf currently yields 2 million barrels of oil daily, about 1 percent of the world supply. Ola Røe

ocean floor), and drilling ships, as well as all types of offshore service vessels including flotels (floating hotels). Tugs made history by pulling the heaviest loads ever moved when rigs made near shore were taken out to sea. Now other Norwegian companies are designing new underwater chambers and robots to eliminate some of the diving work in setting up a rig, and much research is going into the possibility of eliminating the need for large concrete pillars for operations.

The oil industry has become a cornerstone of the Norwegian economy. As exploration expands, the test wells are following the route north from the North Sea off Stavanger to waters off Mid and North Norway—not in the sheltered corridor of the early fishers and Viking traders, but out in the rough waters of the sea.

The East and Southernmost Norway

The earliest division of Norway was between west and east—between the sea and the land as a basic resource; between the fisher and the *bonde* (farmer); between waters flowing to the Atlantic and waters flowing to the Skagerrak. Today, many more Norwegians live in the east than in the west.

The East (Østlandet) faces Sweden and has been much influenced by relations between that country and Norway. The border between the two countries last changed when Norway lost thousands of acres of valuable forests to Sweden in 1658. Some years Norwegian logs could be safely floated down the Trysil River, though it passes the border into Sweden; other years the logs would be confiscated. The capital at Christiania

Norwegian Agriculture

Norway has only three main farming areas—in the southeast, the southwest, and Trøndelag—where there is relatively favorable climate, some flat fields, and fertile soils.

The farms are generally small: on average, 22 acres (9 hectares) of arable land and about 124 ac. (50 ha.) of forest. Following independence in 1905 Norway developed from a mainly agricultural into an industrial country, but as late as the 1950's the government ran homesteading programs to encourage new settlement. There are still government-supported agricultural schools and outreach programs, though agricultural policies are being reconsidered.

Norway's first agricultural school opened in 1825. At that time most farms did not follow systematic methods of crop rotation, but planted the same crop until the field was used up and then turned it into a sheep pasture.

Only 28 percent of all farmers today are full-time farmers. In 1990 there were 94,722 farms in Norway employing about 6 percent of the work force. (In contrast, in 1801, 80.4 percent of the population was involved in agriculture and forestry; in 1865, 64.1 percent; in 1920, 35.6 percent; and in 1960, 19.5 percent.)

(now Oslo) became a significant center during Norway's union with Sweden (1814–1905). The city became even more of a magnet for migration south after independence in 1905. Today the Oslo area, including the counties on either side of the Oslo Fjord, forms the core of modern Norway.

Most farms are dairy farms and produce milk and cheese. Norway has enough cows, beef cattle, sheep, goats, pigs, and chickens to meet its own needs. Potatoes, barley, oats, and wheat are also grown locally, but grains for bread must be imported, as well as sugar and some high-protein feed grains, vegetables, and fruits.

In the past farming was strongly supported by the government at a cost of about 4 percent of the total government budget. The Storting decided in 1976 that farmers in all areas should have the same yearly income as an average industrial worker. Recently these policies are being debated, and subsidies have been reduced.

Some critics have suggested that it might be cheaper to import all agricultural products, but it has long been the government's policy to keep people employed in all rural areas of the country and to maintain Norway's ability to grow much of its own food. The current system of price supports and regulations requiring the sale of property within the family whenever possible is in conflict with regulations being developed within the European Community. Most farmers are against joining the EC, whereas some politicians are debating other ways to support the farmers that might still allow membership.

Old Agrarian Traditions

The eastern valleys and the lands around the Oslo Fjord contain the richest reminders of the farming patterns that evolved through the Middle Ages and became a symbol of Norway's heritage. The importance of farming, the *bonde* way of life, is expressed in the "Peasant Article" of the Norwegian Constitution of 1814. The provision required that two thirds of the seats of Parliament should go to the rural areas and was not repealed until 1952.

Farms used to have a large main house, containing from eight to twenty rooms, and a large number of wooden outbuildings, each serving a particular purpose as a storehouse or cattle shed. These were often raised from the ground to stand above the snow and to protect their contents from mice and rats.

Though the traditional farms and courtyards of East Norway have gone, each area is proud of its local building styles as well as its own folk costumes, which are still worn at weddings and christenings. Some outbuildings are preserved on location or at the folk museums in Lillehammer and on the Bygdøy peninsula in Oslo.

Tracing Family Ties

Some Østlanders trace their families back a thousand years within the same area and have taken their old family farm names as their surnames. From the thirteenth century on landholding was carefully regulated, with the head of household owning land as the representative of a family. Usually only one child inherited the farm and the others went off to sea, to work elsewhere, or, in the nineteenth century, to North America. The child who inherited the farm owed his parents a life pension of food, fuel, and lodging, and a place was also made for unmarried sisters. (Preference was given to sons until a recent law required the farm to be offered to a daughter if she is the first child.) If the farm was sold, the land had to be offered first to relatives, and even if it was sold outside the family, it could be redeemed under certain conditions and recovered by the family. A committee of farmers passes on each sale in their community even today.

Unlike much of Europe, Norway never had a large wealthy landed nobility. There were large and small farms, cotters (tenant farmers), and a few day laborers. While the farming families in the East lived in the valleys, the mountains were an important part of their lives. Traditionally they considered the plateaus and mountains a part of their settlement. There they hunted, fished, and had their summer pastures.

Even today the larger farms are usually in the lower parts of the valleys, where it is easier to use farm machinery. Some of the tiny farms climb up the mountain slopes. *Smaabruker* (small farmers) and *gaardbruker* (big farmers) have their own separate organizations to discuss agrarian and political issues.

The Southeastern Valleys

There are five major valleys. Each runs from the mountains down to the Oslo Fjord, usually with its own river and/or lake system. Each has distinctive features and is separated from the next by unpopulated forested uplands or mountains. The lower reaches of each valley contain small lowland areas that are very fertile. Here small towns, such as Hamar, were founded centuries ago.

The easternmost valley, Østerdalen, is noted for its forests. Norway's longest river, the Glomma, runs through Østerdalen, and the forests climb up to 2,600 ft. (800 m.) above sea level. Cutting and exporting lumber is one of Norway's oldest industries, dating as far back as the sixteenth century in this region.

Wood products today include furniture for domestic consumption and pulp and paper, mostly newsprint and magazine paper, for export. Since the late 1950's loggers have floated less timber to sawmills, and there are hardly any individual farmers who work the forests alone with their horses in winter anymore. Today the forestry industry is highly mechanized, and many smaller mills have been discontinued. A government official quipped: "Now when a tree is cut down, out comes a book."

"Until Dovre Falls"

Gudbrandsdalen, parallel to Østerdalen, is Norway's longest, 124 mi. (200 km.), and largest (15,400 acres) valley, running like a huge crevice between Lake Mjøsa and the Dovre plateau. Its river, Gudbrandsdalslågen, is fed by the melting snows of the Jotunheimen Mountains and has a bright-green color from the glacier as it flows through the meadows. The Dovre Mountains, which separate Gudbrandsdalen from Mid Norway, have become a symbol of Norway. "As long as Dovre stands" is the Norwegian expression for eternity. To show their patriotism, the authors of the constitution of 1814 swore they would be "united and loyal until Dovre falls."

This is the only valley in Norway named for a person: Gudbrand, believed to have been a local chieftain of Hundorp, a center of power during the Viking Age.

The Kings' Highway

The oldest land route connecting southern and northern Norway passes through Gudbrandsdalen on the sunny side—high on the hillside. People have traveled on this highway for more than a thousand years. During the Viking Age, inland chieftains expanded settlements in the fertile valley, clearing lands and building farms. Kings passed by en route to coronations at the cathedral in Trondheim. Monks and pilgrims traveled along it to visit St. Olav's shrine. The passage was difficult particularly during the autumn darkness and rain, the spring floods and landslides, and the winter snows with the sharp Dovre winds.

When Scottish mercenaries hired by Sweden's King Gustavus II in 1612 tried to come through the valley, they were trapped by local farmers who attacked them with a landslide of logs and boulders after a shepherd girl blew her horn to tell them where the enemy was. This incident had an important place in the folk history of the region, for it showed the Norwegians outsmarting the Swedes.

By the 1600's mail carriers made the Kings' Highway their main route. Nineteenth-century playwright Henrik Ibsen (1828–1906) hiked through Gudbrandsdalen and over the mountains to Sogn. His hiking impressions have been linked to some of his plays. In *Brand*, the hero dies in an avalanche near a glacier Ibsen hiked on, and *Peer Gynt* is based upon fairy tales about a folk figure from Gudbrandsdalen. These plays first established Ibsen's reputation within Scandinavia and remain his most popular works at home.

Valley of Artists and Land of Winter Sports

The beauty of Gudbrandsdalen has long attracted writers, painters, weavers, wood-carvers, and musicians. All three of Norway's Nobel prizewinners in literature have ties with Gudbrandsdalen. The novelist Knut Hamsun (1859–1952) was born in Lom. Bjørnstjerne Bjørnson (1832–1910), a playwright, poet, and novelist who was a major figure in Norway's national revival movement, moved to Glausdal in 1874 to live among the freehold farmers for a time and to escape the capital, which he called "Tiger City." Sigrid Undset (1882–1949) lived in Lillehammer, where she wrote novels, many of which are set in the eastern valleys during the Middle Ages.

This "valley of artists" has also long been a major center for winter sports and hiking in all seasons. Lillehammer, 115 mi. (185 km.) north of Oslo, has been chosen as the site for the 1994 Winter Olympics. A pretty and relatively quiet town whose traditions are preserved in the Maihaugen Museum, Lillehammer has hosted numerous sports events since the first national ski competition in 1909.

Numedal and Hallingdal, farther west, and the shorter valleys of Telemark are different from the broader eastern valleys and have been more deeply influenced by the coming of the electrochemical industry and the construction of massive hydroelectric power stations.

The Oslo Fjord: Inventions for Whaling and for Industry

The Oslo Fjord really is not a fjord in the textbook sense, since it is not enclosed by high walls of rock, but it forms a large indentation extending northward from the Skagerrak for over 60 mi. (100 km.). At least one third of all Norwegians live near its shores. At its head, the fjord broadens into a deep-water natural harbor, one of the finest in Europe, and it is here that the capital, Oslo, is located. Along both sides, in Østfold (East Shore) and Vestfold (West Shore), there are several smaller but significant towns. Many of Norway's basic industries are concentrated in the area around the Oslo Fjord, but so too is much of the best farmland in small plains on both sides.

Vestfold is a more varied region than Østfold and has been nicknamed "the Norwegian Riviera," enjoying some of the warmest summers in the country. This climate also supports agriculture, especially orchards. Vestfold claims Norway's oldest town, Tønsberg, a port since the ninth century, next to Sandefjord, formerly an important whaling center. Svend Foyn (1809–1894) invented the shell harpoon there in 1873 after many unsuccessful experiments. The harpoon gun revolutionized the whale-catching industry.

During the following years, Foyn and others undertook many whaling expeditions to the Finnmark coast. In 1904 a law prohibited whaling in those waters because the Finnmark fishers said it ruined their fishing. The Norwegian whalers found other hunting grounds, from the African coast down to the South Pole icecaps. Norway was soon the largest whaling nation. In the peak year of 1930–1931, twenty-seven factory whaling ships were in the Antarctic. In 1986 the Norwegian government placed a temporary ban on whaling (lifted for Minke whales in 1992) except for research, and in 1989 on the hunting of seal pups.

The building of the Norwegian railway system, starting in 1854, with Oslo as the main terminal, helped shift the economic orientation of the country toward the Oslo Fjord and away from the west coast. Cotton- and wool-spinning mills formed the basis of new textile industries along the Aker River in the 1840's, while at the same time engineering firms and machine shops for building ship engines and ship parts were established.

Oslo: At the Center of a Horseshoe

Before it was founded by King Harald Hardrade (Hard Ruler) (reigned 1046–1066) in 1048, Oslo was a small marketplace. In its long history, Oslo has been a religious center, a fort, a port, a manufacturing center, a university town, and finally a capital housing the Storting and King's palace. Oslo's natural setting at the head of the long Oslo Fjord is enhanced by a ring of forested hills that encircle it like a horseshoe.

From a city with 800 residents in 1800, Oslo has grown to become Norway's largest city, with 457,800 in the central city (1990) and close to 800,000 in the metropolitan Oslo area. The main street, Karl Johansgate, bustles with peddlers, sailors, musicians, performing artists, and strollers.

Oslo is home to a number of scientific foundations, several museums

In Oslo's harbor cruise ships, cargo boats, ferries, sailboats, and yachts dock near the Town Hall (right). The renovated section of Aker Brygge (left), a former shipyard, contains many shops and restaurants.   The Royal Norwegian Ministry of Foreign Affairs, Oslo

and art collections—including the Edvard Munch (1863–1944) Museum—and schools of every kind, as well as government offices, corporate headquarters, and the stock exchange.

After Norway was united with Sweden in 1814, King Karl Johan XIV (reigned 1818–1848) ordered the building of a royal palace. He never set foot in it, dying before it was completed in 1848. Ever since, though, it has been the official royal residence. There are no walls or gates to keep any distance between the royal family and the people who enjoy the surrounding park.

The heart of Oslo is Karl Johansgate, with the royal palace and park at the west end and the railroad station at the far east end. In between are the university's first building, the National Theater, the Storting (nicknamed "Lion's Hill" for the lion statues at its entrance), the cathedral, the market square, and many hotels and shops. On May 17, Constitution Day, the whole of Karl Johansgate is crowded with schoolchildren parading with small flags to the palace, where the royal family waves to them from the balcony.

Oslo's Town Hall, a large building with rectangular towers begun in 1931 but formally opened only in 1950, is south of the boulevard overlooking the harbor and includes in the grand hall a massive (85 x 43 foot) mural entitled *The People at Work and Play* by Henrik Sørensen (1882–1962), a leading figure in Norwegian art.

Town Hall has been said to represent modern Norway, whereas Norway's earlier history is represented by Akershus Castle, the oldest remaining structure in Oslo. The castle was built in the early fourteenth century by King Haakon V (reigned 1299–1319).

Oslo is divided east and west by the Aker River, with a score of small waterfalls where early mills and workers' homes were built. Some factories, breweries, engineering shops, and printing presses remain, while others have been renovated into apartments and cafes, including the only women's cafe in Scandinavia to be open every day of the week. The western side contains former mansions; Frogner Park, known for its unusual display of hundreds of sculptures, all created by Gustav Vigeland (1869–1943); and Frognerseter, the summer pastures where farmers drove their cattle on the hills overlooking the city and where today skiers leave the electric trolley on weekends to ski their way back to town. Greater Oslo has a network of ski trails 900 mi. (1,450 km.) long. Many of them are illuminated.

The hills, the river, the fjord and its islands, the parks and squares, make Oslo a very pleasant and comfortable city, simpler and less elegant than some European capitals but in harmony with Norwegian values.

Southernmost Norway

Southernmost Norway (Sørlandet), consisting of the two counties of Aust- and Vest-Agder, is a small area (about 5 percent of Norway), clearly distinguished from other regions by its mild climate, vegetation, and orientation to the Skagerrak—the arm of the North Sea that divides Norway from Denmark about 80 mi. (130 km.) to the south. Kristiansand, the largest town (population 60,000), was founded in

Small towns with many white wooden buildings stand along the indented, forested coastline of low islands and narrow sounds in Sørlandet. Tvedestrand, pictured here, holds a fancy-dress ball in the style of 1812 every summer. Norwegian Information Service, New York

1641 according to plans laid down by King Christian IV (reigned 1588–1648) in order to profit from the strategic position of the southern tip of Norway. At that time it was fashionable to build a town on a chessboard or grid plan with wide streets to prevent fires from spreading. There were a number of fires in spite of this, but the basic plan of a set of ten parallel streets crossed by another set of seven parallel streets still forms the center of the city.

Smaller towns include Grimstad (where Henrik Ibsen worked in a pharmacy in his teens), Risør (known for its annual wooden boat festival), and Arendal. They all enjoyed a boom period during the nineteenth century, when they built sailing frigates and sent them around the world. With the coming of the steamships and the diesel vessels, their trade was lost to the larger ports of Oslo, Bergen, and Stavanger. But since the 1960's boat builders and sailmakers have been supplying vacationers with pleasure boats of small and medium size.

Sørlandet is known for its summer cottages, camping grounds, and harbors along the coast enjoyed by Norwegians and visitors. Here it is warm enough for windsurfing, sailing, fishing, and crabbing. Mandal, Norway's southernmost town, is known for the longest sandy beach in the country. A little farther south is Norway's southernmost point with a lighthouse at Lindesnes.

Kristiansand, and much of Sørlandet, is thought of as the part of Norway that has changed least in the past one hundred years. Behind the coast, woods and hills stretch out for hikers where there are beavers, elk, reindeer, deer, foxes, and hares. There are also small farms where old Norwegian traditions of baking flatbread, fiddling, and crafting silver have been kept up. Near the coast craftspeople make jewelry, glass, and textiles, building on traditional patterns, and artists paint local scenes. Every summer, Sørlandet hosts regattas, museum days, art fairs, traditional country meetings, kite festivals, and fiddle competitions.

Sørlandet is often seen today as beautiful, lively, and quaint. However, life for Sørlanders was often a struggle on small farms (many of which have been abandoned) or on the treacherous seas. This area sent many to North America, and those left behind depended on remittances from American relatives until recently. As a result of the limited endowment of the land, the inhabitants took up fishing, seafaring, and industry at an early date. In the sixteenth century water-powered sawmills were set up, and oak and fir timber was exported. Ships were built and Norwegian sailors went abroad and brought back foreign wives. Iron making also developed, partly to supply chains and anchors and other ironware to the shipbuilders and partly to produce decorative cast-iron as well as wood-burning stoves, which are still found in older Norwegian houses. Metal and chemical industries continue today. Near Arendal Europe's largest silicon carbide plant smelts imported nickel and copper.

Sørlandet faces south and has a reputation for sunniness, but it is also a miniature Norway with a history of diversification: a little agriculture, some fishing, manufacturing, transport, tourism, and other services.

Mid and North Norway

Mid Norway

Mid Norway, also known as Trøndelag (the Trondheim region), holds a central place on the Norwegian map. Some see it merging with the East over the mountains. Others notice the similarities along the coast with the West. Someone in Sørlandet might consider it North, for it is north of the Dovre Mountains, but the real North lies beyond Trøndelag.

Mid Norway has surprisingly fertile farmlands, spruce forests, and accessible coasts. Not far from the coast there are high mountains where thousands of elk, red deer, and wild reindeer run free.

Trondheim, the region's major city, is the third largest in Norway (population 137,000). During World War II the German invaders heavily fortified the harbor and considered moving the Norwegian capital there because of its strategic location.

Consisting of the counties of Sør- and Nord-Trøndelag, Mid Norway is centered around the long Trondheim Fjord. Inner Trøndelag, along the eastern shores of the fjord, is the most favored small agricultural area for its latitude in the world. Here is Norway's largest strawberry-growing area as well as dairy farms. Since the 1960's many owners of small farms have abandoned agriculture and found work in Trondheim while still living at the farmhouse. They lease their lands to larger farmers, who can take advantage of newer farming methods. This process, called dispersed urbanization, is common in Norway, where the transition from rural to urban occupations occurred later than in most countries.

Spruce forests dominate the area north of Trondheim. They produce 10 percent of the annual Norwegian cut—more than any other region outside the eastern valleys. A number of forest industry companies merged in 1988, and Norske Skog now owns the largest paper mill in the country, with an annual capacity of 400,000 tons.

Trøndelag has less industrial development than the East or the West because there are fewer favorable power-station sites, a small population (approximately 377,000) and long distances to larger centers—Trondheim is 340 mi. (547 km.) from Oslo by land and 360 mi. (579 km.) from Bergen by sea. A copper-mining center, Røros, near the Swedish border, was worked until the end of the 1970's. It was founded in 1644, when an elk that was being hunted kicked up clods of earth with a red-gold gleam. The town's old wooden buildings have been restored, and it has been placed on UNESCO's World Heritage List.

Trondheim: Historic Capital

The administrative center of Sør-Trøndelag is Trondheim, whose thousand-year history tells much of Norway's history. A statue of Olav Tryggvason (reigned 995–1000), the Viking King who founded the city,

Norway's three modern kings have been blessed in the Nidaros Cathedral in Trondheim. Here King Harald V and Queen Sonja participate in the blessing on June 23, 1991.
The Royal Norwegian Ministry of Foreign Affairs, Oslo

stands on a tall column in the market square.

In the Middle Ages, Trondheim was an important commercial, administrative, and religious center. Norway's first abbey was built on the island called Munkholmen outside the city, and in 1152 Nidaros, as the city was then called, became an archbishopric. Nidaros Cathedral, the largest and most splendid church in Scandinavia, was paid for from the profits of the trade in furs, fish, and whalebone drawn from Trondheim's northern territories (now the three counties of North Norway). The cathedral is a vivid reminder of Trondheim's place in European history as a major European pilgrimage site (see Chapters VII and VIII). Though the bubonic plague killed off nearly all the population in the fourteenth century and though the political importance of the city faded when Norway became a province of Denmark, Trondheim's central location and rich agricultural surroundings have maintained its position as one of the country's major cities.

Technology Capital

Trondheim has been a research center since at least 1760, when Norway's Royal Scientific Society founded a museum and research station there. The cathedral school, founded by priests of the Nidaros Cathedral, was the country's first seat of learning. In 1900 the local technical school was turned into a technical college, known today as the Norwegian Institute of Technology. A state-funded research institute, SINTEF, has a large research arm that often handles 2,000 projects a year, concentrating on marine and information technology in Norway and abroad. The University of Trondheim (the second largest university in Norway, with 10,000 students) and the national Ship Research Institute are located there, as well as a biological research station with an aquarium. Thus Trondheim is known as Norway's technology capital.

North Norway

North Norway is Arctic Norway, an ancient mountain system of high plateaus, forested in some sheltered areas, and mountains bedecked with small glacial lakes. It is a narrow strip divided into the three counties of Nordland, Troms, and Finnmark, with one of the most complex coastlines in the world—even more irregular than in the southwest. North Norway covers about 35 percent of the country—43,200 sq. mi. (112,000 sq. km.), with a population of about 461,000 (11 percent).

Spectacular nature and a strong regional identity characterize this isolated expanse. The Norwegian poet Nordahl Grieg (1902–1943) said in 1922: "This is the real Norway: freezingly sparse and beautiful." Jonas Lie (1833–1908) is associated with the north. His first novel, *The Visionary* (1870), brought North Norway into Norwegian literature. As one moves north, from Nordland to Troms to Finnmark, the distances between settlements increase and the population density decreases sharply. Nevertheless, people have lived here since prehistoric times. Northerners, including Sami, have supported themselves by fishing, hunting, farming, and eventually by mining iron, copper, zinc, and lead.

North Norway has a frontier quality as an outpost against nature and an experiment in northern adaptation. Level rocky strips close to the shore provide sites for fishing villages and lonely coastal farms in some spots. Ninety percent of the population of North Norway lives within 2.5 mi. (4 km.) of the coast, often in small villages or towns. Hammerfest, close to the North Cape, is the most northerly town in the world (latitude 70°39'48") with a population of 7,600, and in spite of its location has kept abreast of new developments. It got electric lights as early as 1891, when a local official bought an experimental machine at an exhibition in Paris. Hammerfest was also the headquarters of a joint Norwegian-Swedish-Russian survey (1816–1852) to determine the size and shape of the earth.

Inland lie even emptier and wilder landscapes, which are still inhabited by the Sami, some of whom take their reindeer to the coast each spring for better pasture away from the dryness and mosquitoes of the interior.

Due to the Atlantic Current some geographers speak of the counties of Nordland and Troms as only subarctic in character, but in Finnmark (the last and widest county) the impact of the Atlantic Current is mixed with the cold of the Barents Sea to create what has been called "the weather kitchen of Europe." Rain, clouds, mist, and fog are characteristic of much of the Norwegian coast, but gales and squalls add a special quality to the north, which has some of the highest recorded wind speeds in the world. Norway's first meteorological station was established there in 1866. As a government official said, "There is a lot of weather to watch."

"Nature Gone Wild"

The waters and islands off Bodø support one traveler's view that North Norway is "nature gone wild." Not only do the mountains have spectacular shapes, but the tide between islands can be dangerously turbulent. The strait of Saltstraumen between the islands of Straumen and Straumøy links two fjords. The movement of the tide forces a large volume of water through the narrow 165-yard (150-meter) passage, reaching speeds of up to 32 mi. per hour (50 km. per hour) to form one of the fastest tidal currents in the world, creating whirlpools and eddies. A bit farther north of Bodø, off the settlement of Å in the Lofoten Islands, is another whirlpool, the Moskenes.

Bodø is the last stop on the railroad, which arrived only in 1962, linking the city (population 32,000) to Trondheim 453 mi. (730 km.)

south. North of Bodø, the highway extends over 700 mi. (1,100 km.) through Tromsø, the largest city in the north (population 48,000), and on through Finnmark to Kirkenes near the border with the Russian Republic. Parts of the road are closed in winter, requiring either a detour through Finland, a trip on the coastal steamer, or travel by air.

Because drugstores, doctors, and dentists are farther away and extra fuel and clothing are needed, Norway has an *Arktisk tillegg*, an "Arctic subsidy," which the government and some businesses offer their employees, as well as more favorable tax treatment. In addition, the government provides all sorts of services. The University of Tromsø (the world's most northerly university), museums, research centers, and traveling libraries, as well as hospitals and sports centers, demonstrate the Norwegian commitment to provide for all citizens equally, regardless of where they live.

After World War II it was necessary to rebuild most towns in North Norway completely. Kirkenes, which had 7,000 Norwegian citizens and 70,000 German troops, was one of the most bombed cities in Europe. There were 1,012 air alarms and 328 air attacks by the Russians and other Allies. During the Battle of Kirkenes in 1944, hundreds of Norwegians hid and starved in the iron mines for three weeks. The Germans destroyed what was left of the town before retreating.

Crossroads of the North

North Norway has long had an international atmosphere, with its intermingling of Sami, Norwegians, Swedes, Finns, and Russians. The Sami crossed from one territory to another, and Norwegian and Muscovite tax collectors overlapped with each other on the coast for over 400 years. Inland there was a saying that "the Sami pay tax to three kings" (of Sweden, Russia, and Norway). The Eastern Orthodox Church, the Roman Catholic Church, and then the Lutheran Church have met in this northernmost corner of Europe since the fourteenth century, while Soviet submarines have encountered NATO submarines in their annual exercises after World War II.

New Focus on the North

Interest in North Norway is particularly high in the 1990's. The discovery of gas and oil in the Barents Sea has some people now calling the north "The Rich North," though only experimental drilling has begun.

Problems for Puffins

In the recent past one could take a boat or helicopter—Norwegians use them fairly regularly—from Bodø to the Røst Islands to see one of the largest assemblages of seabirds in the world, including some 3 million puffins or sea parrots, as well as rare species such as storm petrels and fulmars, nesting in the high crags. For centuries, seabirds were caught for food, and their eggs provided a highly valued source of nutrition. Before industrial fishing methods came into use, fishers would watch for the seabirds heading out toward shoals of herring, capelin, or other fish and would follow in their boats to find rewarding spots to cast their nets.

At the end of the 1960's, more than 1.4 million puffins nested on the Røst Islands. By 1974 it was clear that a catastrophe was taking place: adult birds were returning to their nesting places with little or no food, and chicks were starving to death in great numbers. Between 1974 and 1983 not a single young puffin survived on the Røst Islands, and the adult population was declining dramatically. Puffin chicks had long survived on the vast quantities of fat herring larvae that drifted north-

Environmentalists, on the other hand, are concerned about the condition of both the Barents and North seas, which are under severe strain.

The boundary between Norway and what was once the Soviet Union used to be heavily and grimly guarded, creating a greater feeling of isolation among North Norwegians. Though these tensions have eased, Norwegians still have misgivings about activities on the Kola Peninsula. While the former Soviet Union was pulling its troops out of Eastern Europe, it moved more and more equipment and forces north to military bases near this border.

---

ward annually just as they were hatching, but people had reduced the herring population to next to nothing.

Chain of Ecological Crises

Once the herring stock was depleted, the Norwegian fishing boats concentrated on capelin fishing farther north. So did the codfish. Soon the Barents Sea was swept clean of capelin, and other seabirds farther north—the guillemots, herring gulls, kittiwakes, Arctic terns, shags, and cormorants—suffered. 1987 was a "black" season for seabirds all along the coast of Finnmark. It was also the year when seals started dying of starvation and invading new territories farther south along the west coast—an example of how the Barents, Norwegian, and North seas are interdependent.

People were shocked because they thought Norwegian waters were especially pure. However, many problems had accumulated: an algae bloom from the south, oil spills, pollution from factories outside Norway, agricultural fertilizers, and the strain from industrial over-fishing. The government has taken steps to reverse this disaster, and though the Barents Sea was still called "the empty sea" in 1990, there are hints of some improvement, and the puffins may have been saved.

A postcard from Kirkenes says, "Stop the death clouds from the Soviet Union," showing the heavy pollution from Russian factories killing the border forests. To lessen pollution, Norway has decided to help the Russian Republic and Eastern European countries modernize their factories. Stopp Dødsskyene Fra Sovjet, Kirkenes, Norway

Norwegian authorities are concerned about the danger of radioactive waste dumps and new Chernobyls from the nuclear reactors on the Kola Peninsula, which are similar to those declared unsafe in Germany. The Norwegian government is stocking iodine tablets in pharmacies throughout North Norway for protection against radioactive fallout from a possible nuclear accident.

Though the North is sometimes seen as a "problem area," natives and newcomers have found strength in their sense of self-reliance and community spirit. Northerners are known to socialize with friends in order to fight the winter darkness (Tromsø has more restaurants per capita than any other town in Norway). They get involved in political activities to remind the government in Oslo of their concerns or participate in committee meetings to plan strategies for the Sami Parliament in Karasjok.

Cod Fisheries: The End of an Era

Life in the North has always been a little harder than elsewhere due to the darkness and sparseness of settlement, but at least Norwegians could always earn a livelihood from the sea, and even in some places from the land. Until this century people on the coast could make a living by fishing and hunting seals and occasionally whales. Some fishers stayed near their own coasts, but many moved seasonally, and their annual rounds included the fishery at Lofoten.

For over a thousand years cod came from the Barents Sea to spawning grounds along the Nordland coast between January and April. The fish was too plentiful to be eaten fresh and was dried on wooden racks in the open air until it was as hard as wood. This "stockfish" was stacked in farmhouses and storage bins, and was sometimes used as bread and to pay taxes.

From Nordland the catch was sent south, via Trondheim and Bergen, to European markets. When cargo boats took the fish to Bergen, grain, salt, flour, spices, cordage, clothing and fabrics, ironware, soap, tobacco, and liquor were bought in exchange. Peter Dass (1647–1707), a Lutheran minister and Norway's first modern poet, wrote simply and affectionately about the lives of his parishioners in his collection called *Nordland's Trumpet*:

> *O cod, you are truly our livelihood nigh;*
> *You bring us from Bergen the much needed rye*
> *And feed Nordland's fishermen amply. . . .*

Should cod-fishing fail us, what then would there be
To buy for in Bergen for you and for me?
Our crafts would be sailing quite empty.

Translated by Theodore Jorgensen

"A Whim of the Codfish"

In the nineteenth century up to 30,000 men flocked to the Vest Fjord, a large inlet between the mainland and the Lofoten wall of islands in Nordland, to participate in some aspect of the Lofoten fisheries. *Lofotfisket* brought together the largest work force in Norway at that time. The visiting fishers would live in very little cold *rorbuer* (cottages) that were often the source of illness and epidemics. The intense activity created a traffic jam of boats until basic organizational guide-

The day of the small fishing boat has passed, and many older fishers in the Lofotens still feel betrayed as they wait for tourists to stop by for a night or for new government plans.   Ola Røe

lines were imposed. Eventually there were such elaborate rules concerning fishing hours and locations for different types of nets that the fishery was called a "state within a state." The fisher's life was precarious. One commentator in 1890 said: "A whim of the codfish, a hurricane in the sky or a cold spring is sufficient to plunge the fishers into distress and poverty."

The Industrialization of Fishing

Originally, all you needed to catch a boatful of cod in the Lofotens was a simple hand line and a small open boat. After World War II there were rapid technological developments with larger boats and improved gear. The most revolutionary "advance" was the introduction of the heavy "purse seine" (a very large net buoyed along the top by corks and weighted along the bottom so that it floats perpendicularly and then closes together like a purse). These nets were more than a mile long and could entrap 600 tons of fish at a single haul. The fish-freezing industry expanded to handle the larger catch, and the quantity of fish caught continued to increase until 1967, when it dropped sharply. In 1947 about 20,000 men took part in the Lofoten fishery and landed over 147,000 tons of cod. Toward the end of the 1980's, only 2,000 men fished, and they brought in 10,000 to 15,000 tons.

The overefficiency of fishing, serious pollution, even the Chernobyl nuclear accident in 1986, and, some think, the limitation on hunting seals have all played a part in causing the fish to disappear. The Norwegian government imposed strict quotas in the 1980's to enable the fishing stock to build up again. Success to some would mean a productive Barents Sea, the source of the cod, and a return of one of Norway's largest cultural symbols: the Lofoten Fishery. But the day of the small fishing boat has passed.

The Norwegian Council for Fishery Research, established after the crisis became apparent, funds research to promote new techniques such as fish farming and to study the interaction between different fish stocks, water temperatures, sea mammals, and fishing quotas. The scientists are developing computer models to try to determine what "sustainable development" could mean for Norway's fisheries. At the same time that Norway is trying to solve these problems at home, it has become a leader in the world environmental movement.

North Norway will always have a wild side; but, to many, that's the way it should be, for there are few places left to wander in the wilderness, something the North can offer to all.

The Age of the Vikings (793–1066)

The Viking warriors and traders, swooping down in their longboats, first put the northernmost corner of Europe on the world map. Historians estimate that they sailed 5,000 mi. (8,000 km.) east-west and 2,500 mi. (4,000 km.) north-south. The Viking Age is usually dated from the first recorded invasion of an English monastery in 793 to the defeat of Harald Hardrade at Stamford Bridge in England in 1066.

While many histories focus on the chronology of violence, trade, and exploration, Norwegians themselves see Viking times as more complex. Some feminists refuse to call all Norwegians of that era Vikings, saying the term should be applied only to the warriors. They emphasize that most Norwegians were farmers and fishers, quietly pursuing their daily lives. Thor Heyerdahl (born 1914) of the *Kon Tiki* expeditions in the

South Pacific points out that Norway was never "a Viking nation," just as "England was not a nation of buccaneers, any more than Spain was a nation of pirates." The Vikings, buccaneers, and pirates were but a small minority of the population.

Older Norwegians remember the Nazis' use of Viking symbols during World War II to try to rally Norwegians to their cause, and they want to stress their country's contributions to a peaceful world instead. But overall, Norwegians have not rejected their ties to the old Viking culture. When oil was discovered in the North Sea, the Norwegians named many of their oil and gas fields after Viking myths and folktales.

Reconstruction of the Viking Age is based on archaeological finds, including runic inscriptions. Runes are Old Norse letters of the alphabet carved on gravestones and objects. Norwegian scholars regularly uncover new remains of Viking market sites at home and abroad. There are also accounts by those whose communities were invaded. These were mostly written by monks, who presented a terrifying picture of the attackers. In addition there are many sagas, stories told by the Vikings and passed on by word of mouth from one generation to another, which were written down in the twelfth and thirteenth centuries. The Vikings are often remembered as warriors who went berserk, eating hallucinogenic mushrooms that made them fight with a wild fury. Scholars continue to analyze all the sources and to broaden the image of the Vikings, and there are ongoing debates about interpreting the size and timing of various events.

Historians note that many Viking settlements were based on trade, were well organized, and showed a high level of architecture and artistry. The Vikings had a "rule of law" in their *ting*s (assemblies), where the people gathered yearly to settle disputes and make decisions. A "law man" was assigned to memorize the laws, and was required to answer anyone who asked legal questions and to recite the

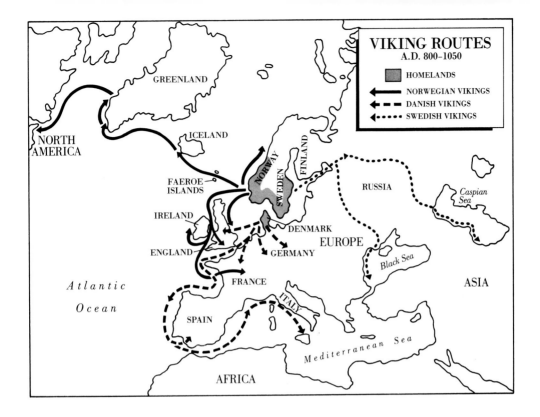

VIKING ROUTES
A.D. 800–1050

HOMELANDS
NORWEGIAN VIKINGS
DANISH VIKINGS
SWEDISH VIKINGS

GREENLAND

ICELAND

NORTH AMERICA

FAEROE ISLANDS

NORWAY

SWEDEN

FINLAND

RUSSIA

Caspian Sea

IRELAND

DENMARK

EUROPE

Black Sea

ENGLAND

GERMANY

ASIA

Atlantic Ocean

FRANCE

ITALY

SPAIN

Mediterranean Sea

AFRICA

laws at the *ting*. Anyone could call a *ting* by sending an arrow to a neighboring farm.

Scholars point out that there was somewhat more equality between women and men in the Viking communities than in the rest of Europe. Women could own property, could divorce their husbands, and were in charge when the men were away. The wife's symbol of authority was the key to the storage chests, which she carried on her belt. The laws from the Viking Age distinguish between free persons and slaves, but not between men and women. Some Norwegians see a connection between the ancient Viking laws and women's strong legal position today. Norway has had an Equal Status Act since 1978.

The Vikings came from Norway, Denmark, and Sweden. Each had different routes of conquest and trade. The Swedes sailed eastward along the Baltic Sea into Russia and eventually south to Constantinople (now Istanbul), while the Norwegians and Danes headed westward and south toward Europe. The Norwegians primarily followed what they called the "western way"—to northern England and Scotland, then southward through the Irish Sea to Ireland and down to Wales. The place names they gave indicate the direction from which they came. They called the Hebrides "the Southern Isles," showing that they came from the north—that is, from Norway or from an earlier settlement in the Orkney or Shetland Islands. To this day the northernmost county in Scotland is named Sutherland, the south land. (See *The Land and People of Scotland.*)

It is impossible to follow the trails of the Norwegians without crossing the paths of Danes and Swedes. For example, Swedes are most associated with "the eastern way," but Norwegians also entered the service of the Byzantine Emperor in Constantinople as members of the Varangian guard (see *The Land and People of Turkey*), and one became commander of the imperial bodyguard. He was the same Harald Hardrade who later became King of Norway and was killed in battle in England in 1066.

The origin of the word Viking is a mystery. Some scholars believe that it meant "creekmen," from the Old Norse word *vik* for creek or inlet. Others think it referred to a pirating center, the Vik, in the Oslo Fjord, thus meaning those who originally came from that part of Norway. Still others suggest the term might derive from the Old English word *wic*, meaning warrior or trader.

The people whose lands were invaded did not differentiate among the Scandinavians. They called them "the men from the North," Norsemen or Northmen, as in the ninth-century prayer "From the fury of the Northmen, deliver us, O Lord." The early raiders, on the other hand, identified with their local districts, calling themselves "men of Hardanger" or "men of Vestfold." Only slowly toward the end of the Viking Age did a concept of national identity, of being "Norwegian," begin to develop.

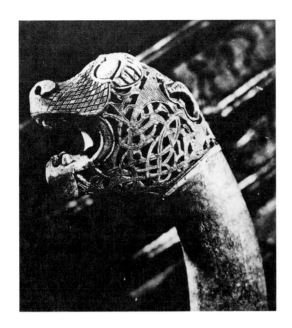

This snarling animal head shows the skill of Viking wood-carvers. Norway continues the tradition of wood carving even today. Norwegian Information Service, New York

Raiders from the Sea

Before the year 800, Norwegians had landed on the Shetland and Orkney islands north of Scotland, and Swedes had set foot on the coasts of Finland and Estonia. In 793 Norwegian Vikings attacked the monastery at Lindisfarne, a small island (3 x 2 mi.) off the northeast coast of England. This raid gave them their reputation for violence. Landing quickly and unexpectedly, a small party of raiders looted the monastery, set it afire, slaughtered many monks, and took others as captives. They sped away in their frightening ships decorated with dragon heads, disappearing over the sea as quickly as they had appeared. Alcuin, an English scholar at the court of Charlemagne, described the shock of this event in a letter: "[N]ever before has such a terror appeared in Britain as we have now suffered from a pagan race, nor was it thought possible that such an inroad from the sea could be made."

1066: Two Views

The year 1066 is one of the most important dates in European history. The Norwegians remember it for the Battle of Stamford Bridge and the defeat of their king Harald Hardrade, while the English remember it for the Battle of Hastings nineteen days later, which brought Norman rule to England. The events involved three of Europe's greatest military leaders—King Harald of Norway, King Harold of England, and William, Duke of Normandy—who fought for control of England.

Harald Hardrade had been King of Norway for twenty years when he asserted a claim to the English throne. With a fleet of more than 300 ships, he crossed the North Sea and landed an army of some 9,000 men in Yorkshire on September 20. Learning of the invasion, Harold of England quickly led his army 200 mi. (320 km.) north and caught the Norwegians by surprise at Stamford Bridge. Their clash was the greatest battle the Norwegians ever fought on English soil. At the end, nine tenths of the Norwegian forces were cut down, and Harald of Norway lay dead.

Three days after the Battle of Stamford Bridge, William of Normandy landed on the southern coast of England with an army of 7,000 men. Once again Harold set off on a forced march with his exhausted troops, meeting William's army near the town of Hastings on October 14. At the end of the daylong battle, Harold of England lay dead, pierced by an arrow. William of Normandy, known in history as William the Conqueror, became the King of England and established a new dynasty (see *The Land and People of France*).

With the defeat of Harald of Norway, the Viking Age came to an end. Since William the Conqueror was a descendant of the Viking Rollo, Norwegians feel a tie to England in spite of Harald's downfall.

Soon the Norwegians were launching more raids against northern England, Scotland, and Ireland. Monasteries were the first targets, because they had much treasure and poor defenses. Pirating forays were followed by bigger and bolder attacks, including large, organized military expeditions, sometimes consisting of hundreds of ships, under the command of a chieftain. In 839, for example, Ireland was attacked by a large fleet commanded by one Thorgils or Turgeis, who founded the cities of Dublin, Limerick, and Waterford.

During the ninth century Norwegians established colonies in Scotland, Ireland, the Isle of Man, and Wales. Along with the Danes, they also looted and burned towns in France, Italy, and Spain. Some believe the Viking leader in Normandy with the name of Ganger-Rolf, or Rolf the Walker (so called because he was so big that no horse could carry him), known in history as Rollo, was a Norwegian, though the majority of his followers were Danes. There is a statue of Rollo in Ålesund on the west coast of Norway, given to the town by the people of Rouen, France, in 1911.

The Viking Puzzle

What led the Vikings to cut down their oak trees, build a new style of boat, and brave the open seas for ten generations? Certainly there were many complex forces, and we can only partially solve this puzzle. Some scholars suggest that the population of Norway, though small, had become too large in relation to its resources because of new migrations from central Europe. Others think that the custom of polygamy, the marriage of one man to several women, which was practiced by the chieftains, contributed to the increase in population. In either case, overcrowdedness could push some to seek land and wealth away from home.

Since the early raids involved only a small part of the male popula-

Old Norse Gods

The mythology of the north goes back long before the Vikings. The Viking poets and storytellers told many tales, sometimes with conflicting details, about the gods and goddesses of the Germanic peoples. The Eddic lays are ancient poems dealing with these mythological gods and heroes.

Chief among the gods were Odin, the god of war and wisdom; Thor, the god of thunder and storms and the slayer of trolls and giants; Freyr, the god of fertility and peace; Tyr, the bravest fighter among them all; and Freyja, the earth goddess and patron of pleasure. Our names for some of the days of the week derive from these Old Norse gods: Odin (or Woden) yields Wednesday, Thor Thursday, and Freyr Friday.

Odin was the god of poetry and magic, as well as war, and the early kings of Norway liked to trace their ancestry back to him. Odin received the warriors who fell in battle at his hall, Valhalla. The hall had

tion, they were an important way for young men to gain status within their families and communities. Raiding was a way to gain a wife. Some captured women as slaves/concubines. Others returned home with stories of their success and enough treasure to give to the bride's family, a requirement of the Viking marriage customs. If a Viking died in battle, he was assured of glory and he believed he would be escorted by warrior maidens called Valkyries to the great hall of Valhalla, where he would fight all day and feast all night.

Some writers speak of "wanderlust" and "the need to know what lies beyond the horizon"—traits that are difficult to pinpoint. The weather

640 doors, each so wide that 960 *einherjer* (the chosen who were admitted to Valhalla) could pass through them side by side.

Odin, who had sacrificed one of his eyes in exchange for a drink from the Well of Knowledge, had two ravens as companions, Hugin and Mugin, which set out each dawn to fly over all the world and came back every night to report on everything that had happened during the day.

While Odin was the chief god, Thor was even more popular because of his power over the weather. His symbol was the hammer with which he made the noise of thunder. Many Vikings wore copies of this emblem as pendants around their necks and took the name Thor as part of their own, such as Thorfinn or Thorvald. Odin's wife, Frigg, the mother goddess, spun gold thread, which was woven into summer clouds, on her spinning wheel.

The myths reflect the ideals of the Viking warriors: courage, valor, and the will to fight. But there are also elements that may reflect Christian influence, such as the good god Balder, the bad half god Loke, and the final doom, Ragnarok.

was another factor, for it warmed up in the ninth century. There was little drift ice and few cyclonic storms, and glaciers melted. These good conditions for long voyages lasted until the twelfth century. In many ways the ocean was regarded as an open door rather than an obstacle. It was a shorter trip to Scotland from Trondheim or the Sogne Fjord or even Oslo, than from Oslo to the northern tip of Norway. Finally, maritime technology played a crucial role. Whether they set out for plunder, land, or trade on their expeditions, the Vikings demonstrated superb navigational and sailing skills. They also designed the right kind of boat.

Long Ships

The Viking ships were slender and graceful, with symmetrical ends and a true keel. They were strong enough to cross long stretches of open water, yet were still light enough to be carried over rapids or to sail in water only a few feet deep. This meant the Vikings could reach places that were inaccessible to the ungainly craft in use by the other seafaring European peoples. The ships could go upriver far inland into the heart of a foreign country or be hauled on open beaches through heavy surf where there was no harbor.

The Scandinavians' most significant innovation was the development of a keel strong enough to cope with the weight of a mast under full sail. The keel, the backbone of the boat, was made from the trunk of a single oak tree. The Viking ship was what is called *lapstrak*ed, or "clinker-built." Clinker construction is a "shell" building technique: That is, after the keel and stem are bound together, a shell of planks is laid, which is then reinforced with wooden ribs. The main feature of a clinker-built boat is the overlapping of the planks, which gives it a "step" form. Even today, the Viking ships are considered the finest examples of clinker construction technique.

The Viking boats were fitted out with one large square sail made of homespun wool with diagonal strips of leather crossing each other to make a diamond pattern and sewn to the cloth to strengthen it. In addition to the one sail, there were oars for auxiliary power. Some of the

A Viking burial ship was found on the Oseberg farm in 1904. Grave robbers had already removed the jewelry but left a 70-foot (21-meter) Viking boat, sleds, dragon heads, and a cart dating from the ninth century. The ship had been used to bury two women, aged about twenty and fifty. One theory is that the older woman is Queen Åsa, the grandmother of Harald Fairhair, the first King of all Norway, and the younger a servant to care for her in the next world. Fully restored, the Oseberg burial ship now stands in the Bygdøy Museum in Oslo. Norwegian Information Service, New York

Modern Oil Fields and Old Myths

Norwegians draw on their rich heritage of Old Norse myths and folk-lore to name many of their oil and gas fields. There is Odin (northwest of Stavanger), Frigg (on the median line between Great Britain and Norway), Valhalla (near the Norway-Denmark divide), and Troll (north-west of Bergen). A field in the north is called Askeladd (lad of the ashes) after the boy hero who outwits trolls in Norwegian fairy tales. There are some fields whose names may be even less familiar to non-Norwegians:

Heimdall (west-northwest of Stavanger) is named for the Old Norse god who guarded the rainbow bridge Bifrost. He was also keeper of the horn that was to signal the doomsday battle of Ragnarok.

Sleipner (close to the median line between Great Britain and Norway) is named for Sleipne, Odin's fastest horse, which had eight legs.

Heidrun (off of Nordland County) is named for the goat that stood on the roof of Valhalla and from whose udders came the liquor the fallen warriors drank.

Gullfaks (west of Sogne Fjord) is a ship in Norwegian folklore that can sail as fast on land as on the sea. In Old Norse myths there is also a horse called Gullfaks that belonged to a giant named Rungne.

Draugen (north of Kristiansund) is the Viking word for a dead person living in a burial mound. In later folktales *draug* came to mean someone drowned at sea who was not buried in sanctified ground and whose appearance was a portent of death. There are many references to *draugen* in Norwegian literature.

warships had as many as thirty pairs of oars and ranged in length from about 65 to 95 ft. (20 to 29 m.). At the stern was a large steering oar controlled by the captain, who stood on the *lypting*, an elevated platform. From the *lypting* he could look down on the crew, direct their attack, and maneuver the ship.

Impressive as these were, they were still open boats, exposing the crew to tumultuous winds, heavy rain, and blinding fog. Each man had his own sea chest, which he used as a seat. Everyone on board worked, slept, and ate in the same cramped place. The sides of the ships were low, and water had to be constantly bailed by hand, especially in rough seas. This was grueling work, and despite desperate effort a ship could be swamped during a storm. To the Vikings, the long ship was more than a means of transport. It served as their home and the basis of their adventurous life. They were even buried in their ships.

Beyond Piracy: Trade and Exploration

Norwegians had been traders from before the Viking Age, and even in the midst of warlike raids there were often truces to permit peaceful commerce. Looking at the map of invasions, one is also looking at a map of expanding trade routes as ships brought products from the far north—furs, walrus tusks for ivory, and dried fish—in exchange for products from as far away as southern Europe and the Orient.

The Norse were the only western sailors in early medieval times who dared to sail beyond landmarks and into uncharted open seas. They carried on trade northward along the coast of Norway and then eastward as far as the White Sea. They discovered Svalbard, the Arctic islands north of Norway. Before the year 1000 they settled all the habitable islands in the North Atlantic—the Shetlands, Orkneys, Faeroes, Iceland, and Greenland, all of which remained in the

The simple beauty of the Viking boat design is imitated to this day in Norway.   Ola Røe

Norwegian sphere of influence for centuries—and landed on the shores of North America 500 years before Columbus.

Settlement of Iceland

The Norwegians began to arrive in Iceland in large numbers in 870. They came from West Norway and from the colonies in the British Isles. Some left Norway to escape the rule of Harald Fairhair (reigned circa 890–940), who became the first king of a united Norway after he successfully defeated a series of local chieftains. But most were farmers looking for land.

Entire families—women, men, children, and babies—set sail with all their belongings, their farm tools, their household goods, and even their animals—sheep, horses, cattle, pigs, and chickens. At the time such animals were smaller than they are today, but the ships were also small by present-day standards. Separated from Norway by some 529 mi. (850 km.) of open seas, Iceland could take three weeks to reach.

Within sixty years, 15,000 to 20,000 settlers had arrived. So many people left from West Norway that Harald Fairhair tried to stop them by placing a tax on emigrants. By 930 all the usable land was taken. This may have led explorers to look for other lands.

Settlement of Greenland

From Iceland, the Norwegians pushed on to Greenland. Erik the Red, a violent but courageous leader, is credited with being the first European to land on Greenland. Erik had been expelled from Norway for murder and gone to Iceland. There he again ran into trouble and committed two more murders, for which he was banished for three years.

Erik decided to spend his exile looking for a land he had heard about. A half century earlier the sailor Gunnbjorn claimed to have sighted new territory to the west when his ship was blown off course. Aside from this sailor's lore, it is also possible that Erik "saw" Greenland before he sailed off. In midsummer the mountains of Greenland can be seen from the hills of northwest Iceland through a mirage effect. Norwegians call this mirage view an *is-blikk*, or "ice glimpse."

Erik's journey to Greenland took place around 981, a voyage that Fridtjof Nansen (1861–1930), himself a great polar explorer, described as "one of the most remarkable in the history of Arctic explorations." In some places his ship was threatened by drift ice every hour of the day and night. Not counting detours into the fjords and inlets of Greenland, Erik sailed about 2,800 mi. (4,500 km.).

Erik spent three years exploring Greenland and then returned to Iceland, where he convinced a group of settlers to go to this new land with him. According to the sagas, Erik decided to call the land "Greenland," even though five sixths of it is permanently under ice, because "people would be the more willing to go there if it had a good name."

Around 986, a fleet of twenty-five ships carrying about 300 people left Iceland and headed for Greenland. Only fourteen boats got through. Nevertheless, two settlements, 400 mi. (650 km.) apart, were established along the fjords of southwest Greenland. Traces of churches and Viking homesteads have been found, as well as a rune stone as far north as 72°55' latitude. Excavations of the remains of what is believed to have been Erik's own farm show it was large and comfortable, with thick walls of stone to protect it against the harsh wind and heavy snow.

At its height, the Greenland colony contained about 3,000 inhabitants. In the twelfth century the Greenlanders got their own bishop after their chieftain sailed to Norway to petition the king, taking a live polar bear as a gift. The colony lasted until the fifteenth century. The king of Norway sent ships to stay in touch with Greenland; but when Norway was merged with Denmark, the Greenlanders were forgotten.

"Vinland the Good"

The colony in Greenland became the springboard for explorations in North America. The seafaring distance between Greenland and Labrador is half the distance between Iceland and Greenland. So once the Norse reached Greenland, it was only a matter of time before they moved on to North America. When the Greenlanders climbed the high mountains behind their settlements and looked west out to sea, they could see the kinds of clouds they usually found above land.

Some scholars believe that other Norse voyagers may have reached the coast of North America before Leif Eriksson. But the sagas give him the honor. Leif, a son of Erik the Red who was called "Leif the Lucky," landed in "Vinland the Good" around the year 1001.

Leif sailed west and landed in several places to which he gave the names Helluland (flat-stone land), Markland (forest land), and Vinland (meadow land). Working from clues given by these names, historians have tentatively identified these places as Baffin Island, Labrador, and Newfoundland. In 1961 the Norwegian archaeologists Anne Stine and Helge Ingstad found the remains of a Viking settlement at L'Anse aux Meadows at the northern tip of Newfoundland, corroborating the saga stories. (See *The Land and People of Canada*.)

After Leif's voyage, there were other expeditions to Vinland, which may have reached as far south as Rhode Island or even Virginia, although no further Viking sites have been uncovered. The sagas recount an attempted voyage by Leif's brother Thorvald and one by Freydis, a daughter of Erik the Red. Scholars believe that as long as the Greenland colony lasted its settlers continued to make short trips to North America to get timber and other supplies.

There was one serious effort to establish a permanent colony in Vinland the Good, led by Leif's kinsman Thorfinn Karlsevne around 1010. His wife, Gudrid, who survived him by several years, was the most widely traveled woman of the age—her voyages had taken her to Norway, Iceland, Greenland, North America, and Rome.

Thorfinn's colony in Vinland lasted three years. When clashes broke out between the Norse and the native inhabitants, the settlers wisely decided to abandon the colony. One of the sagas explains: "They now realized that even if the country was very rich, there would be danger of conflict with the original inhabitants of the country. They therefore made themselves ready to leave and set out on the way to their home village."

Founding the Kingdom

Norway's difficult terrain has tended to keep people apart, and the rivalry of warring chieftains only increased suspicion and hostility. Becoming a united nation was not easy. In the branching waterways and mist-shrouded mountains of the western coast, especially, the residents along each fjord tended to act independently. The fjord region offered the greatest opposition to Norway's first King, Harald Fairhair (reigned circa 890–940).

During the centuries of Viking expeditions, the kingdom of Norway began to emerge. Several districts were joined under a *ting*, or common assembly. One assembly included the fjord districts in the west, another the districts around Lake Mjøsa in the southeast, and a third all the districts around Trøndelag (Mid Norway) and farther north.

The land was split up among various chieftains, who sometimes called themselves earls or kings. As these local leaders began to control larger areas and to extend their power through intermarriage, the more unruly and independent minded went on Viking expeditions overseas, though they sometimes returned to raid their homeland.

Harald Fairhair

At the end of the ninth century Harald Fairhair, who came from a family of chieftains in the southeast, created the kingdom of Norway out of many small chiefdoms. According to legend, a young woman named Gyda urged him to unite the realm, for she refused to marry someone who governed only a small part of the country. She wondered why no one had yet tried to become King of the whole of Norway. Harald accepted her challenge and vowed not to cut his hair until he succeeded, which is why he is called "Fairhair."

Starting from his base in the Oslo Fjord, Harald led a military expedition northward across the Dovre Mountains and won the alliance of the powerful leaders in Trøndelag and North Norway, who accepted his overlordship. The chieftains farther south on the west coast, however, put up stiff resistance. At the naval battle of Hafrsfjord around 900, Harald gained a complete victory over the chieftains of the western fjords. Soon afterward he undertook an expedition to the Shetland and Orkney islands and established sovereignty over them. He made a pact with King Athelstan of England and as a pledge of friendship sent his youngest son, Haakon, to be educated at the English court.

After Harald's reign and right up to the fourteenth century, the kingdom of Norway was an inheritance of his family. For a century after his death, though, the kingdom he had created often seemed on the verge

At Hafrsfjord outside Stavanger a monument commemorates Harald Fairhair's decisive victory that led to the unification of Norway. Stavanger Tourist Board

of disintegrating. At times the country was split up under several chieftains, and at other times parts of it were under the authority of the Danish King. Still, Harald's descendants claimed the kingdom as their legal inheritance, and they fought for it time and again.

The process of unifying Norway was not completed until the late tenth and eleventh centuries, during the reigns of Harald's descendants Olav Tryggvason (995–1000), Olav Haraldsson (1015–1030), and Harald Hardrade (1046–1066). Some historians argue that true unification took even longer and that only in 1130, when the monarchy and the church brought district after district under their rule, could Norway be termed one realm.

Conversion to Christianity

The outcome of the Viking Age was the unification of the country and its conversion to Christianity. During their expeditions overseas the Norse came in contact with the beliefs of Christian Europe. At first some Vikings pretended to convert to get trade benefits, but those who settled abroad usually became Christians. Norway, however, remained faithful to the old gods. Converting the country to Christianity took more than 200 years, and the conversion was accompanied by much bloodshed, more so than in any other Scandinavian country.

Three Missionary Kings

Before his death, Harald Fairhair bequeathed the realm to his son Erik Bloodaxe. Erik's short reign (circa 940–945) was disrupted by continuous battles with his half brothers and the Earls of Lade in Trøndelag who, on and off for over a century, were to be rivals of Harald Fairhair's descendants. He was forced from the throne, and Harald's youngest son, Haakon (reigned circa 945–960), who was only fifteen at the time, returned to Norway and united most of the country again.

Haakon organized the local *ting*s into larger districts and set up a naval defense along the long coastline against the menace of foreign invaders and Viking raiders. The coast was divided into districts, each of which was required to give a warship and crew for the King's use for a certain period of time each year. This system of defense was called the *leidang*. Haakon also organized a method of warnings by means of bonfires on the mountain peaks. In seven days the warnings could reach the whole country.

Haakon, who had been educated as a Christian at the court of King Athelstan in England, was Norway's first Christian King, and he wanted Norway to become a Christian country. The King was so well liked that he was called "Haakon the Good," but he made no headway in establishing Christianity. On the contrary, the people demanded that he participate in their old rituals. The sagas give an account of a feast known as the "blood offering" in which Haakon was forced to take part against his will. The people wanted him to eat the horseflesh and drink the blood in which the flesh was cooked. He refused, but compromised by opening his mouth over the steam. This did not satisfy the people, and at the next sacrifice he was required to eat some of the horse liver.

Olav Tryggvason

Like Haakon the Good, Olav Tryggvason (reigned 995–1000) came from overseas to claim the throne of Norway. As a child this great-grandson of Harald Fairhair had had to flee to Russia with his mother. From there he began a career as a Viking at an early age, conducting raids from the Baltics to the British Isles. He was so famous that he was able to collect large fleets of ships for his part in Viking attacks against England in the 980's and 990's. However, it was also in England that he accepted Christianity and was confirmed by the

Bishop of Winchester under the sponsorship of King Ethelred the Unready—whom he had recently attacked.

When he landed in Norway in 995, Olav was immediately accepted as King in Trøndelag and gradually by the rest of the nation. He founded the city of Trondheim, which he made his capital. Aided by English missionaries, he was determined to bring the Christian faith to the people. Around the year 1000 he sent a Catholic priest with Leif Eriksson on a mission to Greenland to convert the settlers. Leif's father, old Erik the Red, refused baptism, but others accepted. In Norway Olav had more of a struggle. People in Trøndelag and North Norway still believed in the Old Norse gods, and Olav resorted to savage force. Using the brutal methods of a Viking raider, Olav sailed along the coast demanding that the *ting*s submit and accept baptism. Those who refused were tortured or put to death. He forbade the worship of the old gods, destroyed their temples, and built the first church in Norway in a little village called Moster, south of Bergen.

Olav's harsh methods made him enemies. In the year 1000, he and his flagship, *The Long Serpent*, were defeated at the Battle of Svold, the first certain date in Norwegian history. Vastly outnumbered, Olav leaped overboard to his death rather than be captured. Since his body was never found, a legend grew up that he survived and would return some day. Although he was cruel to his enemies, Olav was admired for his bravery and quick wit, and stories of his deeds were passed on from one generation to the next.

The victors divided Norway among themselves. The Earls of Lade controlled part of the country, and the worship of the old gods flourished once again. But Olav's reign had revived the memory of Harald Fairhair and of a united Norway. Soon another Olav, who also could trace his descent back to Harald, fought to regain the kingdom. This Olav, Olav Haraldsson (Olav II), better known as Saint Olav (reigned 1015–1030), is one of the greatest names in Norwegian history.

Saint Olav: Norway's "Eternal King"

According to legend, Olav Haraldsson was waiting in Cadiz, Spain, for fair winds to take him through the Straits of Gibraltar when he dreamed that he was approached by a man who said, "Return to your home, for you are to be King of Norway for time immemorial." On his way home Olav spent the winter in Normandy, and there he was converted to Christianity.

Olav Haraldsson began his Viking career when he was twelve years old. He fought in the Baltics, in western Europe, and in England, where in 1009 he attacked London and helped to tear down London Bridge with grappling irons. This event is remembered in the nursery rhyme "London Bridge Is Falling Down."

In the autumn of 1015, Olav landed in Norway with only two shiploads of fighting men. Within a year he had defeated the Earls of Lade in a hard-fought battle and had himself proclaimed King at the various *ting*s. He extended his rule into parts of East Norway, which until then had been under local kings, and fought the Danes in the Vik area in the Oslo Fjord. By 1020 Olav ruled all of Norway.

Like Olav Tryggvason, Olav II set out to convert Norway—again, at swordpoint if necessary—and in this last struggle between the old faith and the new, Christianity finally won. If the farmers refused to accept Christianity at a *ting*, Olav forced them to change their minds through violence, murder, and fire.

"What a pity it is," the King said when he came down the Otta Valley and looked over Lom, "to have to set fire to so fair a place." The farmers in the Otta Valley accepted Christianity and did not have to see their farms in flames, but that was not true everywhere.

For several years Olav ruled in peace. But the old chieftains resented their loss of power. Finally, with backing from the Danish King Canute, they mobilized against him. The King of Denmark came to

Norway in 1028 at the head of a large fleet, and Olav fled to Russia but soon returned to try to win back the kingdom. On July 29, 1030, at a farm called Stiklestad near Trondheim, the opposing forces met. With the battle cry "Christ's men," but outnumbered two to one, Olav's followers were defeated, and he was killed. His body was secretly carried to the city of Trondheim and buried in the sandbank of the River Nid.

Victory in Defeat

After Olav's death, the Danish King sent his young son Svein with his English mother to rule Norway. This direct foreign rule was unacceptable, and the chieftains realized they had made a mistake. People also began to recall that there had been wondrous signs during the Battle of Stiklestad, and reports of miracles occurring at Olav's grave began to spread.

One year after the battle, Olav was declared a saint. Now Norway had its own patron saint, solidifying its ties with the rest of Europe. Olav was acknowledged as a saint throughout Europe and as far away as Constantinople. Churches were built in his honor by the hundreds, not only in Norway but in Rome and in London, where there were at least six built in his name. The day of his death, July 29, became a great religious festival in the north of Europe. Even today the date is celebrated in Trondheim with reenactments of the battle at Stiklestad and other medieval scenes.

Saint Olav had become both a Christian martyr and a champion of national liberty. Down through the ages, his memory lived on as the symbol of a united and independent Norway. He had become *perpetuus rex Norvegiae*, "the eternal King of Norway." Within five years of his death, two of Olav's former enemies traveled to Russia and brought back his eleven-year-old son Magnus to be King. The foreign rulers

St. Olav's pilgrim's emblem, from about the year 1250, was bought at the cathedral and sewn into a cloak, hat, or bread bag to protect against thieves on the way home and to prove the pilgrim had been to Nidaros. The Restoration Workshop of Nidaros Cathedral, Trondheim

fled the country. The reign of Magnus the Good (1035–1047) inaugurated a new and peaceful era.

Traces of the old beliefs were slow to disappear. Some types of nature and ancestor worship lingered on for centuries, and there was no serious attempt to convert the Sami until the sixteenth century. But after the death of St. Olav, Christianity became accepted as the religion of the country. The old communal beer feasts were incorporated into the observance of holy days. The beer was now blessed and the first cup drunk "in honor of Christ and the Blessed Virgin for good years and peace."

The Saga Kings

Norwegian history from the ninth through the thirteenth centuries is called the Saga Age because it was described in the Old Norse sagas. In the nineteenth century, when Norway was united with Sweden, the sagas strengthened Norwegians' desire to be independent by reminding them of a time when their country was free. The old tales gave the Norwegians a fascinating portrait gallery of their ancestors, many of whom, although violent, were also resourceful and dynamic.

The Saga Age was a time when Norway was developing into a nation state and building its relations with other countries. After the death of St. Olav, new land was cultivated, especially in East Norway, and new towns (Oslo, Bergen, and Stavanger) arose, while older ones like Trondheim and Tønsberg were revitalized.

From then on Norway was recognized as a sovereign kingdom by other countries. In 1038 Norway and Denmark sealed a pact in which Denmark recognized Norway as an independent kingdom for the first time.

Ties with Medieval Europe

With the acceptance of Christianity Norway became more and more linked with the rest of Europe. St. Olav's shrine in Trondheim became one of the great pilgrimage sites of Christendom in the Middle Ages. It was one of the four major centers, along with Jerusalem, Rome, and St. John of Campostella in Castile (now Spain). Thousands of pilgrims from all parts of Europe flocked to Norway each year. Hostels were set up along the pilgrims' route over the Dovre Mountains to accommodate the crowds.

Sigurd the Crusader

Norway's King Sigurd (reigned 1103–1130) led a crusade to the Holy Land in 1108. He fought in Spain, raided all the Arab cities along the coast of North Africa, and helped to conquer the Moslem fortress at Sidon, in Lebanon, which at the time was an important port for pilgrims going to Jerusalem.

When he arrived at the River Jordan, Sigurd tied his kerchief to a stake in the river and challenged his brother, King Øystein (who reigned jointly with Sigurd 1103–1123) in Norway to make the same journey and loosen the kerchief. He presented the booty he had captured during the crusade to the Patriarch in Jerusalem. This is the reason the Lord's Prayer is inscribed in Norwegian, as well as in Hebrew, Aramaic, and Latin, in the temple the Patriarch built on the Mount of Olives.

On his way home Sigurd stopped in Constantinople, where he was lavishly received by the Emperor and where he carved runic inscrip-

Historical Sagas

The word *saga* basically means a "saw" or a saying that deserves to be repeated, but it has come to refer to the prose narratives written in Old Norse during the twelfth and thirteenth centuries and inscribed on sheepskins. They are sometimes called Icelandic sagas, since most were composed in Iceland, although many of them deal with events in Norway.

There are many different kinds of sagas. Some cover the Viking Age, others the settlement of Iceland and life there. Some are works of fiction. Many are historical accounts of various Norwegian kings. The greatest of these historical sagas is Snorre Sturlason's (circa 1179–1241) *Heimskringla* (known in English as *Chronicle of the Kings of Norway*), which is considered a monument of world literature. It is an ambitious work both in its length and conception, for Snorre set out to give a complete history of Norway from prehistoric times down to 1177. The opening words, *"Heims kringla,"* ("The orb of the world"), give it its name. In addition to the sagas and Eddic poems, there is also a body of Old Norse poetry called skaldic poetry. These are poems written by the *skald*s, court poets, who were part of a king's entourage. The poet's function was to entertain the court and to celebrate the important events of a king's reign. Snorre drew on these poems, as do present-day historians, to get a better picture of the kings he was writing about. The poets might exaggerate, but they could not lie outright. As the introduction to the *Heimskringla* explains, "No one would dare to tell the king himself about deeds which everyone present, including the king, would know to be nonsense and lies; that would be mockery, not praise. . . ."

Of all the Icelandic sagas, the *Heimskringla* was the first to be printed, in a Danish translation in 1594. It has had a profound influence in Norway. During World War II Norwegians again turned to the *Heimskringla* to get courage during the German occupation. Today the Norwegians have named one of their oil fields after Snorre.

tions to his own memory on many ancient monuments. He rode home through Europe to great acclaim.

Sigurd and Øystein are known as the "brother Kings." On his return to Norway, Sigurd boasted about his exploits, but Øystein answered that it had been just as noble to remain at home building churches throughout the countryside and leading the kingdom in law and justice. A tradition grew up contrasting the two brothers, one peaceful, the other warlike. In reality they ruled together successfully.

Influence of the Church

The Catholic Church was a great organizing force at home. It is estimated that between the eleventh and thirteenth centuries, 800 to 900 "stave churches," parish churches made of wood, were built. Monasteries were established, bringing new buildings and improved methods of agriculture. The Latin script replaced the old runic writing. Even in Greenland two monasteries were founded. The monks fostered a sense of internationalism, since they kept in contact with their headquarters, no matter how far away they were.

Before the year 1100 the first bishoprics appeared, and from 1152 there was an archbishop at Nidaros (Trondheim) whose jurisdiction covered all of Norway and its overseas territories, including two dioceses in the British Isles—the Orkneys and Man—which had previously been under an English prelate. The church acquired much land and wealth, and the archbishop began to play an increasingly important political part in the country's history.

Civil Strife

The monarchy in Norway was partly elective, for it was the privilege of the *ting*s to proclaim the King. It was also hereditary, but there was no

Stavkirker *(Stave Churches)*

For Norwegians and visitors alike there is nothing so Norwegian as
stave churches, though only about thirty are intact today. The early
churches were quite dark and plain, without pews or a pulpit.
Sometimes the only window was the little one near the altar used to give
communion to people with leprosy, who were not allowed inside.
Leprosy was a major health problem until Dr. G. A. Hansen
(1841–1912), a physician from Bergen, isolated the bacillus in 1873
and freed Norway—and the world—of the disease.

Fascinating large animals and intertwining decorative lines, similar
to Viking wood carvings, decorated the doors, especially the large west
doors, which served as the main entrance. In the middle of the nineteenth century there was a revival of interest in the stave churches, and
a movement for their restoration began, spearheaded by the Norwegian
landscape artist Johan Christian Dahl (1788–1857).

*The earliest stave churches had dragon heads instead of crosses, and carvings some-
times based on stories from the sagas; these were gradually replaced by Christian
themes. This church at Borgund, near the end of the Sogne Fjord, was built around
1150 and retains dragon heads on its upper levels.*   Norwegian Tourist Board, New York

set order of inheritance. Any son of a king, whether oldest or youngest,
whether born in marriage or not—or any brother or other male relative,
for that matter—had a right to claim the throne provided he could get a
local *ting* to back him.

The succession to the throne, which had run smoothly for a century
after St. Olav's death, broke down after King Sigurd's death in 1130 as

various heirs and factions bitterly fought each other. The period 1130 to 1217 is called the Age of Civil Wars. The archbishop and wealthy landowners got together around 1160 and agreed on a new order of succession to try to stop the bloody feuds. They decided the old practice of choosing a king by acclamation at one of the *ting*s was to cease. Instead the King was to be elected by a committee of sixty men, with the bishops acting as an advisory body. This was a tremendous victory for the church.

A new King, Magnus Erlingsson (reigned 1161–1184), was duly elected. He was anointed and crowned by the archbishop in a ceremony of great pomp in Bergen in 1163, the first time that such a coronation was performed in a Scandinavian country. But the grand plans failed.

A new pretender, hailing from the Faeroe Islands, challenged the King backed by the church. His followers were called the Birkebeiner (birchlegs) by their enemies because many of them were so poor that they tied pieces of birch bark around their legs when their trousers were torn. This new leader was Sverre Sigurdsson. He was to be another of Norway's great kings.

"A Little, Low Man from Some Outlying Skerries"

"God sent here from some outlying skerries a little, low man," King Sverre (reigned 1177–1202) said of himself. He promised his followers that each man would be given the rank of the man he killed; he who "slays a thane shall become a thane."

Sverre is considered Norway's most brilliant military tactician. Though heavily outnumbered, he and his ragged troops won victory after victory, constantly outmaneuvering Magnus. He led his Birkebeiner through uncharted forests and over seemingly impassable mountains to launch surprise attacks.

When Sverre became King, he fought the church, which had gained many privileges, and rewarded his followers, who became a new nobility. When he was excommunicated, he defended himself in a brilliant document, "Speech Against the Bishops," in which he argued that the church should be subordinate to the crown. He welcomed poets, saga writers, and scholars to his court.

Sverre commissioned his own saga, which was written by an Icelandic priest who stated in the introduction, "Abbot Karl Jonsson wrote when King Sverre sat over him and settled what he should write." *The Saga of King Sverre* is a contemporary account and is considered one of the leading works of the twelfth century. The Icelander Snorre Sturlason must have recognized its importance, for he did not continue his *Chronicle of the Kings of Norway* beyond 1177, the year in which King Sverre's saga begins.

Birkebeiner and Bagler

The bishops, who were violently opposed to Sverre's policies, formed the Bagler party, a name based on the Norwegian word for a bishop's staff or crosier. The struggle between the Bagler and the Birkebeiner, who by now were wealthy and included some of the leading people in the country, turned into another bitter civil war starting in 1196.

While the conflict was between church and state, between the rights of spiritual and civil authority, it was also a social conflict. The bishops appealed to those who had lost power under Sverre and to those poor who had not been helped by his policies. They also appealed to regional rivalry. The main support for the Bagler party was in East Norway; for the Birkebeiner, in Trøndelag and the West. The conflict lasted even after Sverre's death in 1202. For a time (1208–1217) the country was divided into a Bagler and a Birkebeiner kingdom.

Finally, with the Birkebeiner insisting on him, both sides accepted Sverre's grandson, who became King Haakon IV (reigned 1217–1263). Haakon reunited the country and made peace with the church. He accepted a new rule of succession whereby the throne would pass to the eldest son and once the long period of civil wars ended, both the crown

Knud Bergslien's 1869 painting shows two Birkebeiner rescuing the eighteen-month-old grandson of King Sverre out of Bagler territory. The royal child grew up to become King Haakon IV. Every March skiers in the Birkebeiner Race cross the mountains between Lillehammer and Rena in a difficult 34-mile (55-kilometer) cross-country route carrying 12-pound (5.5-kilogram) backpacks to commemorate the original event.
Vaering Foto

and the church consolidated their power. During the thirteenth century the medieval kingdom of Norway reached its height.

A Norwegian Empire

Haakon IV's reign is called the "Age of Greatness" by Norwegian historians. During his long rule—it lasted almost half a century—Haakon IV, who is sometimes called "Old Haakon," reorganized the government. He established a chancellor and a king's council to advise him and maintained extensive diplomatic contacts with many rulers, exchanging ambassadors and gifts with such monarchs as Louis IX of France and Henry III of England. Haakon sent messengers to the Sultan in Tunisia and made treaties with the Prince of Novgorod (in northwestern Russia) to regulate border conditions in the far north.

The kingdom of Norway reached its greatest extent in the thirteenth century under Haakon IV. The kingdom included all the "western islands" in the Atlantic. In addition, Norway proper contained three additional regions (Baahuslen, Jemtland, and Herjedalen) that are now part of Sweden.

By peaceful agreement Haakon formally annexed Greenland in 1261 and then the commonwealth of Iceland in 1262, which had been independent though with very close ties to Norway. The Pope's representative is said to have complained that it was disgraceful that a country such as Iceland should exist that was not ruled by a king. Both Greenland and Iceland relied on trade with Norway, and Haakon IV promised to send ships and supplies regularly.

The "Law Mender"

During the reign of Haakon's son Magnus Lagabøte (reigned 1263–1280) the royal power continued to grow. Even before there was a state, the Norwegians had had a system of law under the *ting*s. "With law shall the land be built, not by lawlessness laid waste," states one of the old laws.

Magnus got the consent of the *ting*s to revise the laws and persuaded them in the 1270's to accept a common law for the whole country. The law code diminished the rural population's power and increased the King's. It specifically gave the King the authority to "mend the laws." Since the *ting*s were local assemblies, they were in no position to reject any new laws the King might present, or even to offer amendments. The *tings*' acceptance of laws was reduced to registering royal decrees. The old legislative powers of the people were not mentioned in a single word or phrase.

The high officers of the King were now called barons and knights. During the thirteenth century the church and large landowners prospered, towns grew up, and overseas trade increased. In the first year of Haakon IV's reign a trade treaty was made with England, and in the middle of the century with German cities in the Hanseatic League. But the small landholders suffered.

By 1300 only a quarter of the farming land was owned by small independent farmers. Still, Norway did not become a full-fledged feudal society such as could be found in other parts of Europe. The rural cultivators never became serfs. Many had to become tenants on farms they or their ancestors had owned, but they did not lose their personal freedom. British historian T. K. Derry has pointed out that Norway's mountains, fjords, inlets, and valleys were not conducive to knights in armor dashing about the countryside. Farms were scattered, and it was impossible for a lord of the manor to exercise control over them.

Magnus was the last of the kings about whom a saga was written. Only fragments of his saga remain. Norway's far-flung empire was not easy to defend. Scotland had long demanded the Hebrides and the Isle of Man, so much closer to its shores than to Norway. Soon after Haakon IV's death, Magnus sold them to the Scottish crown for a lump sum and a small annual payment at the Treaty of Perth in 1266. Some historians see this loss of territory as a first sign of Norway's decline, which was to become very pronounced in the next century.

CHAPTER IX

Four Hundred Years' Night

In the beginning of the fourteenth century, under the reign of Haakon V (1299–1319), Norway was still a respected power. But it suffered a number of terrible blows in the course of the century that fatally weakened it: The Black Plague had a catastrophic effect, and the German Hanseatic League controlled more and more of the trade and forced out Norwegian merchants. Politically, Norway became intertwined with the other Scandinavian countries through marriage alliances among the royal families and the nobility. Norway's nobles were a much smaller group than their neighbors, and many became part of the Swedish and Danish nobility, losing their allegiance to their own national traditions. When it came time to defend Norway's rights, its nobles sided with Denmark.

Lack of an Heir

The situation that pulled Norway into a union with Denmark that began in 1380 and lasted until 1814 was the fact that Haakon V had no direct heir. This fact set off a string of arrangements that eventually led to a joint throne of Denmark and Norway ruled by Olav Haakonsson (reigned 1380–1387), who died suddenly at age seventeen. "King Olav

The Black Death

The bubonic plague arrived in Bergen in August 1349 and spread quickly along the coast into the fjords and valleys. As the plague moved through the country people spoke of "the Black Death autumn" and "the Black Death winter." The plague came to Trondheim at harvesttime, and swept through East Norway in the winter of 1350, reaching the western parts of Sweden in the spring of that year.

The loss of life was catastrophic. Historians estimate that 25 percent of the population in Denmark and Sweden perished. In Norway the disaster was of even greater magnitude. Half the population died. Some scholars believe that the figure may even be two thirds.

No social group was spared: The clergy, nobles, and farmers all suffered terrible losses. Only one bishop survived. At the end of the fourteenth century there were 60 knights in Norway, as opposed to the 270 there had been at the beginning.

On the small, scattered farms, when there were not enough people to feed the livestock, the animals died, and as a result those who survived the plague faced famine conditions. The devastation was so extreme that Norway did not recover for centuries. Two hundred years after the plague, a quarter of Norway's farms still remained abandoned and

Haakonsson disappeared," the Icelandic annals report. "The Danes said he was dead, but the Norwegians would not believe it." This Olav was the last King born in Norway until Harald V, whose reign began in June 1991.

Olav's Danish mother, Margaret, created a union of Denmark, Norway, and Sweden, known as the Kalmar Union, which officially lasted from 1389 to 1523. She convinced all three kingdoms to accept

overgrown. Whole districts were deserted.

In 1360 the country was ravaged by the "children's death," probably an outbreak of smallpox, and in 1391 yet another unidentified epidemic brought further deaths.

The memory of the Black Death was kept alive for generations. Stories were told of hunters shooting arrows and hitting church belfries, discovering whole parishes that had been lost in the deep forests. A legend grew up about a little girl from Jostedal who was the only one left alive in her community.

As late as the nineteenth century Peter Andreas Munch (1810–1863), who wrote a monumental history of the Norwegian people *(Det Norske Folks Historie)*, stated that the memory of the Black Death still lived "indelibly among the people of Norway."

The epidemic was personified as *Pesta*, a figure dressed in black who roamed the countryside with a rake and broom. When the rake was used, some escaped with their lives. But when the broom was used, everyone died.

Some have compared the Black Death to an avalanche. The calamity swept away all organized community life, leaving Norway ruined in its aftermath, with too few trained people to manage its affairs.

her nephew, a German prince, as King. For the next 400 years Norway was ruled by kings living outside the country, and it was treated as a hinterland.

"Four Hundred Years' Night"

Ibsen called the 400-year union with Denmark Norway's "four hundred years' night." Norway lost its independence, its religion, even its written language. For centuries it seemed that the idea of Norway itself might cease to exist.

Once Norway was united to Denmark, Danish and German nobles were appointed to positions of power. Even when a treaty was signed in 1450 stating that both countries were to be equal, Norway was not treated as an equal partner. In 1536 the Danish Council declared that Norway was to be a province of Denmark "like one of the other provinces . . . and henceforth is not to be, or to be called, a separate kingdom." This marked Norway's lowest political point. However, in the following centuries the terms "the twin realm" and "the dual monarchy" continued to be used to describe Norway and Denmark, so the *idea* of Norway as a separate country was kept alive.

Loss of Overseas Empire

The kings in Denmark paid no attention to Norway's territories, and consequently Norway lost its overseas empire. Christian I (reigned 1449–1481), who was known as "the bottomless purse," lost the Orkney and Shetland islands when he mortgaged them to Scotland for his daughter's dowry in 1469. The sailing of ships to Greenland, which was a responsibility of the King, stopped. After 1476 contact between Greenland and Europe was lost for 250 years. When Norway became independent from Denmark, Greenland stayed under Denmark as if no one remembered Norway had ever had overseas territories.

Norway lost its artisans, intellectuals, and bureaucrats because the only center of the joint kingdom was Copenhagen: from a wood-carver who was taken to Copenhagen to learn to carve ivory to a sea captain who is claimed by Denmark as well as Norway to the writer Ludvig Holberg (1684–1754) who was called "the Danish Molière." Farmers and fishers stayed at home and kept some of the Norwegian folk culture alive, but soon their communities were stripped of their stave churches and they were being preached at in another language— Danish.

Lutheran Church Imposed

In the same year that the Danish Council declared Norway a province of Denmark, the King also declared that the Lutheran Church, financed and controlled by the government, was to be the religion of the land. In 1536 the Catholic bishops of Norway were dismissed or imprisoned, and King Christian III (reigned 1536–1559) ordered the Archbishopric of Trondheim to be subdued by force. The new Lutheran bishops were placed under the authorities in Copenhagen. All the Catholic Church's property was taken by the crown and given to Danish nobles.

The Lutheran faith did not begin to be accepted until after 1600— and even later among the rural population. Farmers at first refused to let the new ministers bury their dead and continued to bless their fields and observe the old saints' days.

Works of art and manuscripts were plundered from monasteries and churches; many of them ended up in Copenhagen. Some stone churches were torn down to provide building material for fortifications in Denmark. The archbishopric was abolished, thus destroying the Norwegian church's national center. The cathedral in Trondheim

Hamar Cathedral, dating from the twelfth century, was destroyed by fire in 1567 and never rebuilt. The ruins stand on a small peninsula jutting out into Lake Mjøsa, Norway's largest lake. The Chronicle of Hamar, *written about 1550 by an unknown Catholic writer, gives a sad picture of Norway's plight when Danish rule was felt in the local parishes.* Norwegian Information Service, New York

fell into ruins, a symbol of what was happening to the country. Seventeenth-century Danish tax collectors wrapped their account books with priceless thirteenth-century Norwegian literary documents.

Loss of Written Norwegian

In most countries when the Protestant religion replaced the Catholic faith, the new religion strengthened native traditions. The Protestants insisted that church services be conducted in the language of the people rather than in Latin, and the Bible was translated into the vernacular. But in Norway the Lutheran Church, coming from Denmark, forced the Danish language on the people.

The Danish and Norwegian languages had evolved in separate directions since the days of the Vikings. By the sixteenth century Danish sounded foreign to Norwegians. Yet all the church services—the sermons, the hymns, the catechism the children had to learn by heart—were in Danish.

Danish became the only accepted language. All government affairs and instruction were carried on in Danish. Anyone wanting to read books had to learn that language. In the 1550's Denmark, Sweden, and even Iceland had printing presses. There were none in Norway. Anyone who wanted to publish a book had to go to Copenhagen, and the book had to be printed in Danish.

Ordinary people continued to speak Norwegian dialects. But as Danish came to be the language of the educated, this caused deep social divisions. The natural evolution of written Norwegian stopped, although it had existed earlier than written forms of Danish or Swedish, with consequences that are still felt today in the two official Norwegian languages.

Failed Rebellions

Peasants revolted many times during the Dano-Norwegian union, but their rebellions were severely crushed. When Sweden successfully rose up against the Danes around the year 1500, Knut Alvsson mounted a similar national rising in Norway. He captured the castle of Akershus in Oslo and occupied the royal seat in Bergen. But he was murdered by the Danes at a peace negotiation carried on under a promise of safe-conduct. This treachery was commemorated by Ibsen in a poem, "At Akershus," in which he said: "Knut Alvsson's death blow was a blow at Norway's heart."

The last champion of Norwegian independence in the later Middle Ages was Olav Engelbrektsson, the last Archbishop of Trondheim. He used any and all means to fight Danish supremacy—diplomacy, secret negotiations, sabotage, and even military force. The bishop built a castle along the Trondheim Fjord, hired troops, and secured warships. Finally, when promised help from the Holy Roman Emperor Charles V did not arrive, the archbishop realized he had lost. Olav Engelbrektsson sailed from Trondheim in 1536 and died in exile in the Netherlands the following year.

Caught Between Denmark and Sweden

The sixteenth through the early eighteenth centuries was marked by constant warfare between Denmark and Sweden as each tried to become the major power in Scandinavia and to dominate the Baltic. Among the many wars were the Seven Years' War (1563–1570), the Kalmar War (1611–1613) and the Great Northern War (1700–1720). The tax burden for these wars fell heavily on Norway, which contributed twice or even three times as much to the Danish treasury as Denmark paid out for Norwegian defense.

"Farmers' Peace Treaties"

Many Norwegians were willing to fight only in defense of their country. Throughout the sixteenth and seventeenth centuries farmers on both sides of the Norwegian-Swedish border regularly made secret agreements that they would not attack each other. Such agreements were known as "farmers' peace treaties."

When Norway was invaded in the early years of the eighteenth cen-

Since King Haakon V built the castle of Akershus in Oslo, it has played a prominent part in Norway's history.   The Royal Norwegian Ministry of Foreign Affairs, Oslo

Peter Wessel Tordenskiold (Thundershield)

Both Denmark and Norway celebrate the famous deeds of the Norwegian-born naval hero Peter Wessel. The son of a Trondheim merchant, he had run away from home at fourteen and made his way up to the position of admiral.

Wessel was made a noble under the name of Tordenskiold (Thundershield) after capturing a Swedish admiral and a thirty-gun frigate in 1715. The following year, with a squadron of seven ships, he sailed into Dynekilen, a short fjord in Sweden, and destroyed the entire Swedish fleet. He was killed in a duel at the age of thirty.

tury by Charles XII of Sweden, Norwegian soldiers fought successfully. Charles XII was determined to make Fredriksten, the border fortress at Halden, a Swedish fortress. Despite heavy attacks, the Norwegians kept him at bay. He was shot, probably by one of his own soldiers, in 1718 during the siege of Fredriksten, and the war ended abruptly.

Norway had proved its ability to defend itself in a dangerous situation. Norwegians had also played a major part in defeating Sweden at sea. The daring naval exploits of the Norwegian Peter Wessel (1690–1720), in particular, aroused the enthusiasm of the whole country. He was seen as a latter-day Olav Tryggvason. As a result of the Norwegians' conduct during this war, their prestige rose.

Signs of Recovery

In the sixteenth and seventeenth centuries Norway at last began to recover economically from its decline. Trade increased, especially in lumber, due to the invention of the water-driven saw, which revolutionized the processing and export of timber. Prior to the 1520's, planks had been cut by ax and split by wedge.

Fish remained Norway's main export, and the fisheries greatly expanded. The appearance of huge quantities of herring off Norway's coast added to the traditional cod fisheries of the North. The power of the Hanseatic League had declined, and with the development of the herring industry the Norwegians came into their own.

Iron, silver, and copper mines were opened in many places in Norway's vast mountain areas. The silver works in Kongsberg were founded in 1624 and the copper works in Røros in 1644. Shipbuilding yards were erected on the south coast, and Norway became a seafaring country again. By the middle of the eighteenth century Norway had nearly 600 ships, many of them quite large.

The countinghouses of the Hanseatic League were at Bryggen, the part of Bergen overlooking the harbor.   The Royal Norwegian Ministry of Foreign Affairs, Oslo

A sign of recovery was the increase in population. In 1500 Norway's population was not more than 180,000. By 1665 it is estimated that it had grown to about 440,000.

"Norway, Nursery of Giants"

By the eighteenth century, a movement of national revival was beginning. Owners of timber yards and ironworks, and other prosperous merchants, pressed for greater independence for Norway in economic affairs. Their main demand was for a national Norwegian bank. Intellectuals in Denmark compared the plight of the peasants in Denmark who were still serfs with the free Norwegian farmers and held them up as a model. Historians began to encourage research into the Old Norse language and Norway's medieval past. The Royal Scientific Society, founded in 1760, promoted studies that would benefit Norway.

The Norwegian Society in Copenhagen, organized in 1772, became a rallying point for Norwegian students who drank to the toast "Norway, Nursery of Giants." Norway had no university. Norwegians who wanted to get further education had to study at the University of Copenhagen (established in 1479). "Has a country like Norway no right to enlightenment, and can this be obtained without a university?" asked Bernt Anker, a wealthy Oslo shipowner and merchant.

The demands for a Norwegian university and for a national Norwegian bank came to symbolize the growing national consciousness. These demands were repeatedly denied, since the Danish government feared any move that would give Norway more freedom.

After a large sum of money had been collected in Norway, permission to establish a university was finally granted in 1811 (during the Napoleonic Wars of 1807–1814, when Norway was blockaded and could not be administered from Copenhagen).

Whirlwind of the Napoleonic Wars

Throughout the Napoleonic Wars, Denmark's and Norway's sympathies were divided. Denmark was allied with France, whereas the Norwegians would have sided with England, with which they had strong trade ties.

When Denmark declared war against England in 1807, there were terrible repercussions in Norway. The British blockade of the Norwegian coasts brought all shipping to a standstill. No supplies of foodstuffs reached the country. There were bad crops in 1808 and again in 1812 ("the black year"). Norway suffered country-wide starvation.

Napoleon was defeated at the Battle of Leipzig in 1813. The victors agreed that Sweden, which had joined the coalition against Napoleon, should be given Norway to safeguard its western border and as compensation for having lost Finland to Russia in 1809. (See *The Land and People of Finland*.) At the Treaty of Kiel (1814), Denmark was forced to cede Norway to Sweden. The old Norwegian dependencies of Iceland, Greenland, and the Faeroe Islands were not included in the transfer and thus came under exclusive Danish rule. The 434-year union of Norway and Denmark ended.

Sweden was not to maintain the same control over Norway as Denmark had. Even before the union with Sweden began, Norwegians took a major step toward independence.

Reestablishing Nationhood

In the nineteenth century Norway reestablished its nationhood and laid the foundations for the progressive social democracy it became in the twentieth century. The fight for national identity was seen on the political level in the constant clashes between the King and the parliament. Culturally, the national revival unleashed a torrent of ideas and art work, out of which such outstanding figures emerged as the playwright Henrik Ibsen (1828–1906), the composer Edvard Grieg (1843–1907), and the painter Edvard Munch (1863–1944). Norway's population tripled, even though thousands emigrated to America. After 1840 the economy expanded, especially in the fishing, shipping, and forest-product industries.

Contemporaries called 1814 *annus mirabilis*—the astonishing year.

In early January Norway was under the rule of an absolute monarch and all important decisions were made in Copenhagen. By the end of the year it had its own capital and a completely new political system.

Events of 1814

When news of the Treaty of Kiel giving Norway to Sweden became known, there was shock and anger. Peace was welcome, but it was insulting for Norway to be treated as a spoil of war. The King could abdicate the crown of Norway if he wished, people felt, but he had no right to cede it to a foreign country.

A spirit of rebellion against the treaty quickly spread, aided by Prince Christian Frederik, the nephew of the Danish King, who was governor of Norway. The Prince's first plan was to have himself proclaimed King. This idea met firm opposition. Instead he would have to be elected.

At a private meeting of the Prince and a small group of influential Norwegians on February 16, known as "the 1814 Assembly of Notables," Prince Christian Frederik was declared regent, and he then called for a general election to a national assembly. All Norwegian men were to meet at church services to elect delegates and swear to "defend Norway's independence and sacrifice life and blood for their beloved native country."

The Eidsvoll Assembly

One hundred twelve delegates met in Eidsvoll, about 40 mi. (60 km.) from Oslo on April 11 at a manor house belonging to Carsten Anker, a wealthy land and factory owner who was one of Christian Frederik's closest advisers. The roads were in poor condition and a spring thaw made them almost impassable, yet delegates reached their destination on time. A majority were relatively young public officials, though one third were farmers.

A small group led by Count Wedel Jarlsberg (1779–1840) favored union with Sweden. They were suspicious of Christian Frederik's motives, which they saw as an attempt to reunite Norway to Denmark. As far back as the 1770's, some Norwegians had had secret consultations with Swedes in the belief that the country would be better treated under Sweden than Denmark.

National Romanticism

While politicians were asserting Norway's political rights, artists and intellectuals were seeking out what was especially "Norwegian" in the country's natural setting and folklore, as part of the Romantic movement that swept through Europe in the early nineteenth century.

Collectors made heroic efforts to record folktales and folk songs, fairy tales and ballads, proverbs and nursery riddles, in numerous different dialects. They took careful note of folk costumes and dances, while painters such as Johan Christian Dahl (1788–1857) and Adolph Tidemand (1814–1876) depicted the grandeur of the Norwegian landscape and scenes of peasant life on their canvases.

The leading figures in the collection of folklore were Peter Christian Asbjørnsen (1812–1885) and Jørgen Moe (1813–1882), who began to publish their *Norske Folke-Eventyr* (Norwegian Folktales) in 1841. These stories became an important source for artists, illustrators, and writers and are still read in Norway today. As in Ireland, folklore has

The vast majority of delegates, led by Christian Magnus Falsen (1782–1830), a county judge in the Oslo region, wanted immediate and total independence. Falsen was made chair of the committee that drafted a constitution.

Eidsvoll Constitution

The Norwegian Constitution of 1814 drew on the United States Constitution, the French Constitution of 1791, and constitutional practices

had a strong influence on Norwegian literature and identity.

Scholars researched Old Norse mythology and literature, still others Norwegian history and prehistory. Clergymen, educators, and bureaucrats became amateur archaeologists and archivists looking for new insights from Norway's past. Some ideas were farfetched (including the idea that *all* Scandinavians and Germans were descended from a north Norwegian people), but many helped to assemble and preserve records later used by trained historians.

Nationalistic enthusiasm went into the Landsmål (later Nynorsk) movement, which opposed Danish influence on the spoken and written language. (See "Bokmål vs. Nynorsk," Chapter II.) Some of the Landsmål advocates also became involved in a movement to try to regain Norwegian control of Greenland.

In the 1850's Bjørnstjerne Bjørnson and Henrik Ibsen began to write under the momentum of the idea that an independent people must produce a national literature. (See Chapter XV.)

in England. It established the principle of the sovereignty of the people and the separation of powers among an executive, a judiciary, and the legislature, called the Storting for its associations with the Old Norse word *ting*. On May 17 the delegates adopted the Constitution, which was the most democratic in Europe at that time. As its first act, the assembly elected Christian Frederik King.

Sweden refused to accept the actions of the "men of Eidsvoll." The great powers—Great Britain, Austria, Prussia, and Russia—insisted the promises they had made to Sweden were to be kept. At the end of July Swedish troops attacked Norway.

After two weeks of fighting, Crown Prince Karl Johan, who had been one of Napoleon's generals before accepting the Swedish crown and changing sides, initiated an armistice and a political compromise: Sweden promised to accept the Eidsvoll Constitution. Christian Frederik promised to abdicate as soon as the Storting met. He left Norway on October 10, and on November 4 the Storting elected the King of Sweden as the new King of Norway. A new union had begun.

From the Norwegian point of view, the short period of independence brought significant gains. The union with Sweden was based on the acceptance of the people's representatives, not on the Treaty of Kiel. Most important, the Eidsvoll Constitution was saved. The two countries were to have one king and stand together in war, but in all other respects they were to be independent of each other in full equality.

Uneasy Union with Sweden (1814–1905)

The two countries had different views of what the union meant. Sweden had hoped to incorporate Norway as a replacement for Finland, and Karl Johan's aim was to merge the two kingdoms gradually. The Norwegians, on the other hand, wanted to preserve as much independence as possible. The struggle between the monarchy and the Storting began almost at once and lasted throughout the ninety-one-year union.

Constitutional Power Struggles

The main conflicts throughout Norway's union with Sweden focused on constitutional issues between the Storting, which fought to protect Norwegian rights, and the King, who tried to expand Swedish authority. The Storting acted from the very beginning to limit the King's prerogatives. It voted to abolish the nobility (in 1815, 1818, and again in 1821 when the bill became law), partly to prevent the King from winning supporters by creating more nobles.

King Karl Johan introduced bills to amend the Constitution throughout his long reign (1818–1844). These were always rejected, in the end without even being discussed in committee. More and more the Constitution came to symbolize Norway's freedom and independence, and attempts by the King to change it were seen as almost sacrilegious.

Democratic Trends

As the century progressed, more Norwegians became involved in the political process. The Storting became more representative in the 1830's when farmers started to elect members from their own ranks instead of public officials and lawyers. Ole Gabriel Ueland (1799–1870), a small farmer from southwestern Norway, became the leader of the farmers in the Storting. Another major reform was the establishment of local self-government in 1837.

Political parties slowly took shape. Small farmers and intellectuals began to organize and hold meetings. They became the Liberal Party, calling themselves Venstre, the left. Landowners, merchants, and gov-

Battle of the Marketplace

During the 1820's people in the cities, students, and sometimes also representatives of the Storting began to celebrate Constitution Day. The King tried to ban all such activities. Karl Johan called a special session of the Storting in January of 1828 in which he personally attacked the Seventeenth of May. That year the holiday was not celebrated.

May 17, 1829, was a warm and beautiful day in the capital. People flocked to the wharf to see the paddlewheel steamer *Constitution,* which had been ordered from England. The ship was greeted with hurrahs and national songs. In the afternoon about 500 people gathered in the public square to enjoy the good weather. Around nine P.M. the chief of police ordered a force of cavalry and infantry to clear the streets. Several people were ridden down.

The event caused a national outrage, since the population had been peaceful and done nothing unlawful. The young college student Henrik Wergeland (1808–1845) had his jacket split open by a saber cut. He sent his torn jacket to the commander of the fortress of Akershus in a basket as a protest. From then on Wergeland became associated with May 17.

After the "Battle of the Marketplace," the Storting issued an address to the King, defending the celebration of the Seventeenth of May as a right belonging to the people. Karl Johan finally abandoned his opposition.

ernment officials formed an alliance that became the Conservative Party. They called themselves Høyre, the right. Both were registered as national political parties in 1884. Workers formed the Labor Party in 1887.

"Now and For Ever"

A struggle arose over the role of cabinet ministers. The Liberals wanted the cabinet to be responsible to the Storting rather than to the King. They fought for the introduction of parliamentarianism—that is, the principle that the executive branch of government, in the form of the cabinet, must have the support of the national assembly if it is to remain in power.

A bill authorizing cabinet ministers to take part in the deliberations of the Storting was passed with increasing majorities in 1874 and 1877. The bill was intended to open the door for parliamentary government, but the King refused to accept it.

Nineteenth-century interest in the nation was translated by some artists into an interest in the Norwegian peasant or farmer. Erik Werenskiold (1858–1938), in his painting Peasant Funeral, *reminds the viewer of the hard life led by most rural Norwegians.*
Norwegian Information Service, New York

When the union with Sweden was dissolved, Norway was enjoying a period of economic growth due to the expansion of shipping and the development of hydroelectric power from its waterfalls.   Ola Røe

When the amendment came up for the third time, the issue was joined. According to the Constitution, a bill becomes law without the King's signature if it passes three times in separate sessions of the Storting. The Conservatives argued that the King had absolute veto power in cases of constitutional amendments. The Liberals disagreed. Throughout Norway people followed the situation with mounting interest.

In 1880 the Storting passed the bill and declared it valid. The cabinet refused to obey and did not appear in the Storting. Only the Court of the Realm (made up of some members of the Storting and the judges of the Supreme Court) could decide if the cabinet had been right to disobey the Storting.

The election of 1882 focused on the constitutional crisis, and it was unsurpassed in Norwegian history for its passionate intensity. The writer Bjørnstjerne Bjørnson gave the Liberals their battle cry: "In Norway the Norwegian people shall be master, they and no one else, now and for ever." The Liberals won overwhelmingly.

In the spring of 1883 the charges against the cabinet were drawn up. The Court of the Realm, now packed with Liberal Storting members, impeached the ministers. The King gave way and appointed a cabinet headed by Liberal Party leader Johan Sverdrup (1816–1892), a brilliant lawyer and orator, called "a phrasemonger" by his opponents. Since that time Norway has had a system of parliamentary government. Under Sverdrup's administration (1884–1889) more Norwegians were allowed to vote, the army was made more democratic, and trial by jury was introduced. The elementary school system was also improved.

Dissolution of the Union with Sweden

One feature of the union placed Norway in an inferior position from the very beginning. The Norwegians did not have a foreign service of their own. Foreign affairs were handled by the Swedish King and his cabinet in Stockholm. By the end of the nineteenth century the Norwegians' demand for their own consular service was not only a matter of prestige. It made economic sense.

During the century Norway's merchant fleet grew rapidly. The Industrial Revolution in Europe and America created an ever-increasing demand for transportation, and Norway's skippers and shipowners took advantage of the opportunity. The result was that Norwegian businesses and exporters were directly competing with Swedes in some areas and could not count on the Swedish consuls to look after their interests.

This question of an independent Norwegian consular service brought about the final break with Sweden. Norway spent the final years of the century building up its military power. The navy was enlarged, the army was given modern artillery, and along the Swedish border new fortresses were constructed.

The Storting passed a resolution for the establishment of an independent Norwegian consular service in 1892. It did so again in 1905. Prime Minister Christian Michelsen (1857–1925) showed quick-wittedness in the intricate maneuvers that followed and became a national hero.

The King vetoed the bill as expected. The Norwegian cabinet refused to countersign the veto and handed in their resignations. Prime Minister Michelsen argued that according to the Constitution, the King could exercise his royal functions only through a cabinet approved by the legislature, which he now lacked. Therefore he was no longer King and the union had ceased to exist. On June 7 the Storting declared the union with Sweden dissolved.

A referendum to determine whether or not the people wanted to remain in the union was held in August 1905. The Norwegians voted 368,392 to 184 to end the union.

After independence most Norwegians applauded the presence of English-born Queen Maud and Crown Prince Olav. Norwegian Information Service, New York

Independence

When Prince Carl of Denmark was offered the throne of Norway, his father-in-law, Edward VII of England, urged him to accept immediately. Carl declared that he wanted to know where the Norwegian people stood first. In a new plebiscite in November 1905, Norway voted in favor of a monarchy over a republic by a large majority (87.9 percent), and the Storting unanimously elected him King. On November 25, 1905, the new King, who adopted the name Haakon VII (reigned 1905–1957), arrived in Norway with Queen Maud and their young son, who was renamed Prince Olav. With the name Haakon, the King reestablished a connection with the old line of Norwegian kings that had been interrupted for 525 years. For the first time since the decline and fall of medieval Norway, Norway was once again a truly independent nation.

World Wars
I and II

Norway dissolved the union with Sweden in 1905 without bloodshed. There had been no fighting on the Scandinavian peninsula since the eighteen days of warfare in 1814, and the newly independent Norwegians felt safe in their part of Europe, which was already known as "the peaceful corner." After gaining independence, Norway's major aim was to stabilize its political democracy and modernize its economy.

One concern was the fact that about 30 percent of shares in Norwegian businesses were owned by foreigners. Some members of the Storting complained that foreigners were buying waterfalls and other real estate to run chemical and metallurgic industries. The debates between conservatives, opposed to regulations, and liberals, favoring control of outside investors, were remarkably similar to debates in

1970–1972 concerning the impact of possible membership in the European Economic Community (EEC).

In 1917 the Storting passed a Concession Act imposing various controls on foreign investment, including production fees to be paid to the Norwegian government. These same regulations turned out to be important for dealing with foreign concessions in the North Sea oil bonanza in the 1970's.

Traditions of Neutrality

In foreign affairs Norway pursued a policy of neutrality. As far back as the 1890's there had been a strong pacifist movement advocating world peace through negotiation. Military leaders were not highly regarded in Norway.

During World War I Norway was neutral, but as a shipping nation it had trouble maintaining that role. Norway had to negotiate trade agreements against blockades and embargoes by the Allies and faced German submarine warfare, from which it suffered heavy losses. Over 900 Norwegian merchant marine ships were sunk and more than 2,000 sailors perished.

Norway came out of World War I as a nonbelligerent nation with its territory intact, and the belief in neutrality was strengthened. The war created a boom for the nation's exports, but the wartime inflation was worse than elsewhere, and fiscal mismanagement at local and national levels had disastrous results. The interwar years were filled with a rise in bank failures, unemployment, and labor strife. In the 1920's and early 1930's, Norway lost more hours to strikes than did any other Scandinavian nation.

The Norwegian Labor Party, which was closely associated with the trade union movement, took a temporary radical turn, calling for a workers' revolution, and was the only social democratic party in Europe to participate in the Communist International set up in Moscow (1919). By 1923 the party rejected the strong role Moscow expected to play in Norwegian matters and withdrew. Since then the Labor Party has become a socialist reform party, stressing the need for full employment and social services. From 1935 to 1963, without interruption, the Labor Party was in the majority in the cabinets, giving Norway the longest-lived socialist government in Europe at that time.

Clouds of War

As tensions increased in Europe during the 1930's, Norwegian leaders reemphasized their determination to remain out of any war that might erupt. This was also the view of King Haakon and Queen Maud, but they knew Norway was walking on a tightrope in a tornado. In reality, many Norwegians assumed that Britain would protect them in the event of war.

As the danger of German ambitions became more apparent, Norway began a modest program of defense spending, but it was too little and too late. In 1940 the Norwegian army numbered 17,000. The navy consisted of 57 small ships.

When World War II began in September 1939, Norway had had 126 years of peace. It immediately declared its neutrality, but that declaration was of little significance. Both Winston Churchill, then First Lord of the Admiralty in England, and his counterpart in Germany, Grand Admiral Erich Raeder, recognized the strategic importance of the Norwegian coast.

Norway had excellent bases from which German submarines could operate in the North Sea. It was also a major route for the supply of Swedish iron ore, a vital raw material for Germany's armaments industry. A portion of the iron ore was sent by railroad to the ice-free

Norwegian port of Narvik and then shipped along Norway's territorial waters to Germany.

On April 8, 1940, the Allies announced that the British navy had laid mines along Norway's coast to halt the shipments of iron ore. Norway protested. The next day it faced a far worse crisis.

Operation Weserübung

Before dawn on April 9, 1940, Germany invaded Norway and Denmark. Norwegians over fifty years old still remember the bombers emblazoned with swastikas flying overhead. The surprise attack, code named Weserübung, had been carefully planned months before and was brilliantly executed. It was the first time in military history that large numbers of troops were transported in warships and that aircraft carried troops right to the scene of the fighting. Denmark capitulated within a few hours. Norway decided to fight.

At Oscarsborg Fort in the Oslo Fjord the German ships encountered heavy fire from the fort's aged guns and torpedoes. The large cruiser *Blücher* with 1,600 aboard was sunk, and the battleship *Lutzow* was badly damaged. The Germans broke through and captured Oslo, but they had been delayed a few crucial hours.

The sinking of the *Blücher* gave the government time to react. The King and members of the cabinet and Storting left the capital by train early in the morning and went to Hamar, some 80 mi. (130 km.) to the north. The gold of the Bank of Norway—fifty tons in 1,542 boxes—was loaded onto twenty-three trucks, which also headed north.

Elverum Authorization

In the afternoon of April 9 the Storting met in Hamar. The session was interrupted by news that German troops were approaching, and the

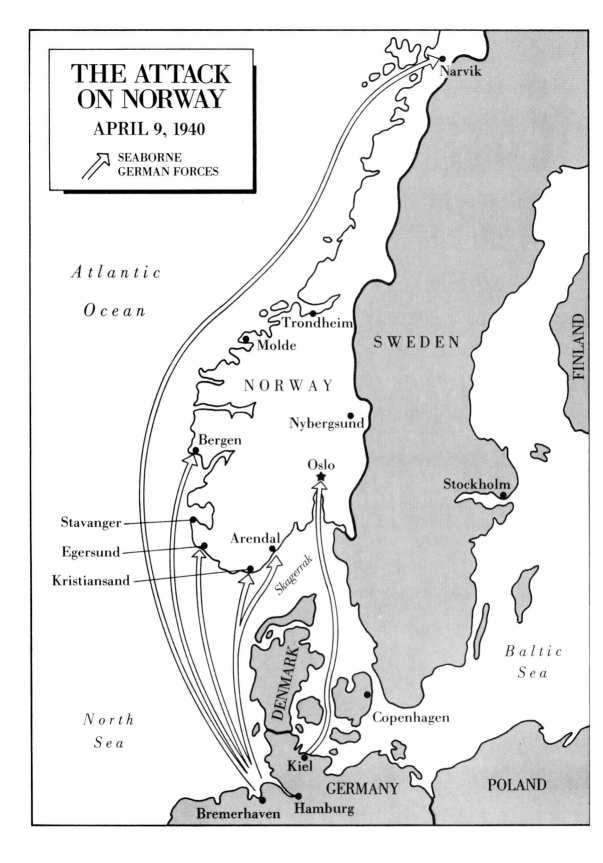

THE ATTACK ON NORWAY

APRIL 9, 1940

↗ SEABORNE
GERMAN FORCES

Narvik

Atlantic

Ocean

Trondheim

Molde

SWEDEN

NORWAY

Nybergsund

Oslo

Bergen

Stockholm

Stavanger

Egersund

Arendal

Kristiansand

Skagerrak

Baltic
Sea

DENMARK

North
Sea

Copenhagen

Kiel

GERMANY

POLAND

Bremerhaven   Hamburg

FINLAND

members fled to Elverum, a few miles to the east. Here the Storting made a far-reaching decision. Unanimously they decided that the government should have full powers to act for the nation, even if the King and cabinet were forced to leave Norwegian soil. Further, the government was empowered to retaliate against the invaders using all necessary means. The Elverum Authorization, as it came to be known, provided the legal basis for the continuance of the Norwegian government-in-exile.

Haakon VII's Stand

Germany demanded that Norway surrender and that King Haakon appoint Vidkun Quisling (1887–1945) to be Prime Minister. Quisling was the founder of the small Norwegian Nazi party, the Nasjonal Samling (NS) (National Unity). King Haakon refused. He declared he would rather abdicate.

Immediately after this rejection, the Germans bombed Elverum and the tiny village of Nybergsund close by in an attempt to kill the King and Crown Prince and paralyze the constitutional authorities. The officials hid in the woods nearby. The inhabitants of Nybergsund still recount the story of their sixty-eight-year-old King sitting in the snow, urging the people not to despair.

Always just a step ahead of the advancing German troops, the King and cabinet made their way across Gudbrandsdalen to the west coast, pursued by bombers. The American ambassador's military aide was killed by bomb fragments. On April 29, while Molde was in flames, the King boarded a British ship that took him north to Tromsø. There, on May Day, the provisional capital was set up.

King Haakon VII's stand inspired the Norwegians and stiffened their will to resist. He became the symbol of resistance throughout the war.

Fighting Back

Norway fought for two months, which was impressive for such a small country. Norwegian forces continued fighting in North Norway until early June. Britain and France sent troops and with Norwegian soldiers recaptured Narvik, the first victory against Germany in World War II. The British fleet inflicted heavy losses on German warships. For a few heady days the Allies hoped that the northern third of Norway could be held.

But the military situation in western Europe was desperate. On May 10, 1940, Germany had advanced into Holland and Belgium. France was on the verge of falling. On June 7, 1940, the King, the cabinet, and what was left of the Norwegian navy and air force were evacuated to Britain. Norway would continue the war against Germany from London as an Allied power.

Throughout the war, the letter H and the numeral 7 appeared on mountainsides, snow-banks, and city walls. A youngster seems frightened by his daring act of painting the sign, declaring that the King lives on.   Norway's Resistance Museum, Oslo

The name Quisling entered the world's vocabulary as a word for a traitor after he volunteered to be Prime Minister of Norway under Hitler's regime. AP/Wideworld Photos

"Look to Norway"

Norway was occupied right up to Germany's capitulation in 1945. The Germans set up a government under Reichskommissar Josef Terboven (who committed suicide at the end of the war) and later under the Norwegian-born Quisling (who was later brought to trial for treason and executed). Membership in the NS increased from a few thousand in August 1940 to a high of 43,400 in November 1943 due to constant pressure to join. But even at its largest, party membership was under one percent of the adult population.

Because Hitler was convinced the Allies would invade through Norway, he sent heavy reinforcements. Eventually there were 400,000 German troops in Norway, which at the time had a population under 3 million. Food supplies were short throughout the war. The Germans commandeered 40 percent of Norway's annual production.

In December 1942 U.S. President Franklin Delano Roosevelt called Norway "conquered and unconquerable." "If there is anyone who still wonders why this war is being fought," he added, "let him look to Norway. . . . If there is anyone who doubts the democratic *will* to win, again I say, let him look to Norway."

Acts of Resistance

After the war Norwegians referred to the years of occupation, 1940–1945, as "the five long years" in ceremonial speeches and everyday conversation. Their opposition was expressed in countless acts. Some protested symbolically by wearing paper clips (a Norwegian invention) on their cuffs and collars, by tracing the emblem of Haakon VII while skiing, by wearing flowers in their lapels on patriotic occasions, and by refusing to ride buses where they would have to sit next to Germans or NS members. These acts often resulted in imprisonment. Others hid radios, which were forbidden, so they could listen to BBC broadcasts from London. Some helped write and distribute underground newspapers, of which there were sixty by 1943.

"Sports Strike"

One of the first mass reactions to the Nazis was the so-called "sports strike," which began in the autumn of 1940. The new German-led Ministry of Labor and Sport set up a state-controlled Sports Union, to which all teams would belong. The result was a national "sports strike" that lasted for the duration of the war. All sports organizations discontinued their activities. Members of sports clubs became the nucleus of the secret underground army, Milorg, that prepared for liberation, training and stockpiling weapons in uninhabited mountain hideouts. At the end of the war, the membership in Milorg numbered about 47,000.

Norway's national institutions—the courts, church, and educational system—fought nazification and upheld democratic principles. All the judges of the Supreme Court resigned in December 1940. The bishops and most of the clergy of the Lutheran Church resigned. Teachers refused to sign a loyalty oath. Over a thousand were arrested, and the schools were closed for a time.

Norway's many cultural and business organizations outwitted the Nazis. The moment they were under Nazi control, people resigned from the organizations, which ceased to exist or barely functioned. The leaders and many members went underground and formed secret action committees. These developed into a vast, invisible network of civilian resistance that was eventually organized in coordination with the government-in-exile in London.

Underground Resistance

At first the resistance was loose and informal, but eventually those involved in secret activities against the Nazis were organized as the *Hjemmefront* (Homefront). From the very beginning some Norwegians warned individuals of impending arrests and set up transportation and escape routes. About 50,000 fled across the border to Sweden to save their lives or to join the Norwegian armed forces in Britain. About 3,300 escaped in fishing boats, yachts, or even rowboats across the North Sea.

Among the escapees were a little over half of Norway's very small Jewish population. The Resistance never issued a call to help the Jews, although there were many individual acts of humanitarianism in helping those who did escape. Of the approximately 1,400 Norwegian-born

Communication Through Fish Crates

Thirty-five thousand Norwegians were arrested and held in several concentration camps and prisons. The largest was Grini, on the outskirts of Oslo, which also served as a transit camp for the approximately 9,000 Norwegians who were sent to concentration camps in Germany, Austria, Poland, Czechoslovakia, and France.

A fish seller in Oslo, who was responsible for supplying fish to the camp kitchens, was allowed to reuse his fish crates because there was a wartime shortage of packing cases. The crates became an important tool for the resistance. Hollows on the corner posts of these crates were soon filled with messages sent in and out of the strictly guarded prison. In other situations microphotographs were smuggled out in toothpaste tubes to Sweden and then to London.

Jews and 200 Jewish refugees from central Europe, 763 were deported and killed at Auschwitz and other death camps. Only 24 of the deported Jews survived.

Shetland Bus Service

Norwegian fishing boats of all sizes joined the "Shetland Bus Service" that ferried escapees to Scotland and returned to Norway with weapons, radios, and special agents. News of German troop and ship movements were sent by secret radio transmitters. The British also parachuted arms and supplies into Norway. All this work was dangerous and led to frequent arrests or flight of the resistance people. The

Germans retaliated by shooting or imprisoning a great many Norwegians after any commando raid or act of sabotage.

Rjukan Heavy Water Plant

The most important act of sabotage was the destruction of the heavy-water (deuterium oxide) plant at Rjukan in Telemark, needed by the Germans in their race to build an atomic bomb. On the evening of February 27, 1943, nine Norwegians trained in Great Britain climbed down a steep and icy mountainside, crossed a river, and climbed up another mountain to the heavily guarded factory. They eluded the guards, broke into the factory, poured out the heavy water, and planted explosives. They fled unseen. Despite the 3,000-man search mounted by the Germans to comb the whole area and make arrests by the dozens, four remained safely hidden on the Hardanger Plateau, while five of the saboteurs skied 250 mi. (400 km.) to the safety of Sweden.

A Fighting Ally

King Haakon VII and his cabinet were only one of several governments-in-exile in London, but Norway had important advantages. The rescue of all the gold reserves—some boxes were loaded onto small fishing vessels that got caught in crossfire—made the government financially independent, as did the revenues from its merchant marine.

With these financial resources the government was able to support the resistance and reequip its naval, air, and land forces to operate with those of the Allies. As early as the autumn of 1940, four ships of the Norwegian navy were patrolling the Arctic Ocean for the Allies. Norwegian military units took part in the naval campaigns in the Atlantic, in the combat following the Allied invasion of continental

"Little Norway" was established in Toronto, Canada, to train Norwegian pilots.
Norwegian Information Service, New York

Europe in 1944, and in the air combat over Britain and Europe. Crown Prince Olav was the Supreme Commander of the Norwegian Armed Forces.

One Million Extra Soldiers

Norway's merchant marine, which consisted of more than 1,000 ships, made the most important contribution to the war effort. One of Quisling's first acts on April 10, 1940, was to order all Norwegian merchant ships to report to German, Italian, or neutral ports. Not a single captain followed those orders. They all went to work for the Allies under the control of the government-run Nortraship with headquarters in London and New York.

Norway's merchant ships helped save Great Britain during the Battle of the Atlantic in 1941. Norwegian tankers brought the oil with-

The merchant marine has reason to look tired. The work of supplying the Allies was dangerous. Half the Norwegian ships were sunk, and 3,600 sailors lost their lives.
Norway's Resistance Museum, Oslo

out which the island nation could not have survived. The merchant marines participated in all the Allied landing operations, including those in the Pacific. Norway's merchant fleet was said to have been worth a million extra soldiers.

Joining NATO

Upon Germany's defeat in 1945 King Haakon returned home to a deliriously happy welcome on June 7, 1945—five years to the day after his departure. Norway came out of the war with honor and increased prestige.

Disagreements between the Soviet Union and the western powers broke out almost immediately in the postwar years. The Communist takeover of Czechoslovakia in 1948 had a strong impact on Norwegian public opinion. Their anxiety was further sharpened when Finland was forced to sign a mutual assistance pact with the Soviet Union (see *The Land and People of Finland*). Moscow sent several threatening notes early in 1949 reminding the Norwegians that they shared a border. A later note asked for a nonaggression pact.

Norway's experience in World War II showed that it could not rely on neutrality, nor did Norwegians believe that Sweden's proposals for a separate, nonaligned defense alliance among the Scandinavian countries would work. Norway joined NATO (signing the North Atlantic Treaty, which provided for a collective defense against a possible attack by the Soviets or any other aggressor) in April 1949 and NATO's northern headquarters were located near Oslo.

Reconstruction and Economic Recovery

Norway was left impoverished by the war and occupation. There was an acute housing shortage, since no building had taken place during the five years of occupation. In the Northern counties all houses, buildings, and harbor facilities had been destroyed by the retreating German troops.

The Labor government was given very wide powers to rebuild the economy. There was a lot of belt tightening, including food rationing, but by 1949 Norwegians were beginning to eat better. Norway received Marshall Plan aid (organized by the United States to help European countries after World War II), which provided an extra margin. By the beginning of 1953 the North was rebuilt, the merchant fleet was larger than before the war, and hydroelectric power had increased 50 percent.

Norway made a solid recovery. The nation was already prosperous in the 1960's before the discovery of oil.

Democratic Traditions

The twentieth century has witnessed a quiet social revolution in which Norway was transformed from one of the poorest countries in Europe into a strong social democracy with an extremely high standard of living. This change began as Norway gained its political independence and sped up its economic expansion, culminating in the tapping of gas and oil reserves on the continental shelf. Another important change has been the rise of women in politics, especially apparent since the 1980's.

Women: Left, Right, and Center

Norwegian women are used to making decisions. In many rural communities men used to go fishing off the coast for several months, leaving the women to run the farms and local affairs. The pattern continues today, with men going off to work on the oil rigs for two or three weeks before returning home for a similar period, but the difference is that now there are also women working on the rigs, and most women on-shore are no longer on the farm.

In farm communities in the past a young woman was often alone during the summer months tending the sheep, goats, and cows at a *seter* and had the freedom to develop relations with a young man and sometimes start a family, while her suitor was waiting for his father to retire from the farm.

Norway was the second country in Europe to give women the vote in national elections (in 1913), seven years after Finland. But until 1945 no woman had been a cabinet minister, and Kirsten Hansteen was then given the title of Consultant Minister without a department to run. Still, the principle that at least one woman should be a member of each cabinet was established.

Norwegian women were later than other Scandinavian women to enter the paid labor force. Even in the 1990's there are strong patterns of occupational segregation, differences in pay, and major discrepancies in the sharing of housework. Few women hold high-level jobs in industry or banking.

Nonetheless, especially in government, there has been a major explosion in the role of women. The Equal Status Act of 1978 was amended in 1988 to require that the number of women on all publicly appointed committees and boards must be at least 40 percent. This example of what Norwegians call "positive discrimination" has led political parties and other organizations to follow suit. In the 1990's the three major political parties, of the left (Labor), center (Center), and right (Conservative), are headed by women.

Norway has established the world's first Department of Women's Law at the University of Oslo and a major Secretariat for Women and

Norway's first woman Prime Minister, Gro Harlem Brundtland, was elected in 1981 and was returned to that post in 1986 and again in 1990. Norwegian Information Service, New York

Research that sponsors studies of current and historical issues such as the role of Harriet Backer (1845–1932), Norway's most important woman painter, and the early fighters for the vote such as Gina Krog (1847–1916) and Frederikke Marie Qvam (1843–1938).

Commitment to Social Welfare

Norway has used its wealth to build a modern and substantial social welfare system that is consistent with its old traditions. In Viking times some regional *ting*s passed statutes providing for relief of poor persons. King Magnus the Lawmender's national code in the thirteenth century placed the primary responsibility for the poor with relatives but also provided for community assistance called the *legd*. The *legd* was a legal obligation requiring every farm to take in the poor for a short period on a rotating basis. The *legd* continued into the nineteenth century. With the Poor Law of 1845, local governments were charged with caring for orphans, the sick, and the aged.

Within rural communities a certain amount of sharing of wealth was built into such customs as "going a-begging"—when a poor bride and groom spent their honeymoon visiting from farm to farm and collecting presents for their household, and when carolers and "star boys" (who performed a Christmas play about the Wise Men in some communities) could demand handouts, which were sometimes money, though often only cookies. Memories of past hardships partially account for Norwegians' desire to have state-provided security.

Support Through the Life Cycle

Norway's National Insurance Scheme includes a basic package of health care, paternity and maternity leaves, pensions (adjusted to the cost of living), unemployment insurance, job-training programs, subsidized aid for the handicapped, homes for the aged, home assistance for families in need, refuges for battered women, and so forth. Norwegians do not have to worry about the economic consequences of illness, injury, or pregnancy. Norwegians live a long, generally healthy life (female life expectancy is 79.6 years, male life expectancy 72.9 years), which has put some pressure on nursing homes.

Individuals, employers, municipalities, and the state contribute to the national insurance plan that provides these benefits. Though there are not enough nursery schools and kindergartens—in 1991 there was a waiting list of 12,000 in Oslo—the government has set improvement of child-care arrangements by the year 2000 among its top priorities.

Before the late 1960's many young people had to leave home if they wanted education beyond the required seventh grade. Now there are schools in all municipalities through the ninth grade or higher, and 90 percent of students completing junior high school continue on to high school. There are also many opportunities for tuition-free higher education in one of the four universities (at Oslo, Bergen, Trondheim, and Tromsø) or in the newer regional colleges.

Increased educational opportunities helped change Norway from a nation with many farmers and factory workers to one with many technicians, professionals, and service workers. Children of industrial workers, clerks, and salespeople became teachers, social workers, and health-care professionals. Some Norwegians fear that this rate of upward mobility cannot continue through the 1990's.

The Ombud System

The Storting has established a number of different Ombud offices to see that citizens are heard if they have grievances against the government and its various agencies. There is an Ombud for Equal Status questions; a Civil Ombud to hear complaints about public administration; another to listen to conscientious objectors, among others. Norway was the first country to establish an Ombud for Children (in 1981), which includes The Children's Hotline, a free telephone service for children to call and leave a message with their complaints or questions.

The social welfare system has evolved through both legislation and labor negotiations. By 1935 unions, often associated with the Labor Party, agreed to meet with employers' groups and the government in annual or biannual negotiations. These negotiations among labor, management, and government have continued with a reasonable degree of agreement to this day. Farmers and fishers are also organized in cooperative associations that negotiate with the government concerning regulations, pricing, and price supports (subsidies).

Although there are many private businesses in Norway, the government is involved in many decisions—concerning subsidies, the regulation of foreign investments in Norwegian businesses, and extensive public purchases of commodities and services. There are also state regulations concerning paid vacations, restrictions on overtime, and employer-employee relations. For example, all major changes, such as plant closings, must first be discussed with the employees. Finally, the government has a monopoly on the railroads, the sale of alcohol, and several mines; owns the petroleum giant Statoil; and is part owner (51 percent) of such major Norwegian companies as Norsk Hydro, which is involved in metals, chemicals, and oil exploration.

Norway has no shoe shiners and very few panhandlers. If Norway has any group that approaches affluence, it is the richer shipowners

Norsk Hydro's Karmøy plant, the largest aluminum factory in Western Europe, is representative of Norway's electrometallurgical processing industries. As Norway approaches the twenty-first century, industrial jobs are declining (16 percent of Norwegian employment in mid-1991) while jobs in the service sector are increasing (40 percent of the work force in mid-1991). Norsk Hydro, Karmøy, Norway

and their families, but they feel they are overtaxed. Taxes and family allowances cut the difference between the high earners and low earners a good deal, leaving some critics to suggest that the differences in salary are not significant enough to motivate workers. Lately support has increased for politicians who promise to reduce taxes, as the gains of a new political party, the Party of Progress, indicate. The principle of equality is very important to Norwegians. But the social welfare system in which economic differences are balanced by services provided

Walking with Kings

The King and the royal family are Norwegian symbols of social stability, political continuity, and the unity of the people. They cannot be brought before a court or removed from office. Since 1905 the royal family has had a tradition of being close to the people. King Haakon VII (reigned 1905–1957) took as his motto in 1905 "My All for Norway," and each King since has done the same.

Though few thought that the affection for Haakon VII could ever be matched, King Olav V (reigned 1957–1991), who was already respected as a resistance hero, soon became equally admired for his personal touch and hard work. One might meet him skiing outside Oslo without bodyguards, and during an oil crisis in 1972, when the nation was asked to conserve fuel, King Olav took the trolley to go skiing and insisted on paying his fare. He represented Norway with dignity and humor and made his weaknesses public. For example, he had a slight case of dyslexia, which caused him problems when he read speeches. But since it was known, his struggle became a symbol of human strength.

Norway was without a Queen from 1938 to 1991. The first queen, Maud (1869–1938), had been frail most of her life, although she was a

by the government may have to be modified as Norway adjusts to the major changes in the European marketplace.

Of Farmers and Kings

There is an old saying in Norway: "If the farmer has money, everybody has money." This principle of equality in many versions has long been a theme in Norwegian politics. Prime Minister Gro Harlem Brundtland

gracious hostess and sportswoman. She was the daughter of King Edward VII and Queen Alexandra of Great Britain and died in London. Crown Princess Martha, Olav's Swedish-born wife, assumed the duties of First Lady of Norway, but she died in 1954 before her husband succeeded to the throne. So the nation was particularly happy when Sonja Haraldsen, born a commoner, and the wife of Olav's son Harald, became Norway's first Norwegian-born Queen in 1991.

In addition to royal duties and interest in political affairs, the royal family in each generation has been active in sports, especially skiing and sailing, and involved with social concerns.

Despite royal reluctance to influence public policy, King Olav made a strong statement in 1987 in favor of maintaining an open society for the increasing stream of refugees and reminded his country that he had arrived as a two-year-old immigrant when most of his kin were abroad. Princess Martha Louise (b. 1971) was appointed a goodwill ambassador by the High Commissioner for Refugees at the United Nations in 1991. On the ecological front Harald V was president of the World Wildlife Fund before becoming King and often stresses the serious need for conservation worldwide and Norway's special situation as a country with untouched wilderness areas.

(b. 1939) has compared the Norwegian emphasis on equality with the American emphasis on individual freedom as a basic assumption rarely questioned.

In Norwegian fairy tales, the King is not a very regal figure but rather a good-natured farmer shuffling about in slippers, a man other farmers could approach as an equal. A few Norwegians have seen the monarchy as a contradiction of the ideal of equality, but most point out that the King was *elected* in 1905. Until 1935 the Labor Party was unfriendly to the monarchy, sometimes refusing to pass the palace budget or to attend dinner parties with the King.

World War II was a turning point in the acceptance of the monarchy, and though Ibsen said of his compatriots, "Norwegians can agree on only one sole point, to drag down what is most lofty," when a proposal to make Norway a republic was introduced in 1990, it received only the 17 votes of the Socialist Left Party and two from the Labor Party in the 165-member Storting. Over 90 percent of the country approves of the royal family today.

Newcomers to Norway

Some Norwegian feminists have spoken of "the unfinished democracy" with regard to the status of women. In the 1990's "unfinished" may be as appropriate a description of the integration of foreigners into Norway. Foreigners amount to only about 3 percent of the total population. The majority are from the other Scandinavian countries. About 40 percent of foreigners are from outside Europe, especially Asia. In the 1960's Norway accepted migrant workers, most of whom were from Pakistan, India, Turkey, and Morocco. A number of them became small shopkeepers in Oslo. Since 1975 the government has placed a ban on immigration.

Asylum Seekers and Refugees

As other European countries started restricting their policies on political asylum, Norway received a large increase in asylum seekers, for which it was not prepared: from 150 in 1980 to 8,600 in 1987. Many came from Chile, Iran, Sri Lanka, Yugoslavia, Poland, and Somalia. At the same time Norway was also accepting an annual quota (between 1,000 and 4,000) of refugees through the United Nations High Commission for Refugees, most recently from Iran and Vietnam. While almost all were accepted on humanitarian grounds in 1987, the acceptance rate has since dropped.

Norway provides schooling in the native language as long as at least four students are interested. Newcomers are also expected to learn Norwegian and attend school if of school age or be integrated through work programs and Norwegian-language classes. Some refugees have been placed together outside of Oslo; for example, Tamils from Sri Lanka worked together in fish-filleting plants in North Norway in 1990. However, most live in Oslo or near Bergen and Stavanger.

Although Norwegians have a very good humanitarian record for projects abroad, many are uncomfortable with the foreign-born population and overestimate its size and impact on society. Some individuals have encountered discrimination and tension. The government, media, and members of the royal family try to combat the hostility, while various groups have founded associations to celebrate their cultural heritage and educate others. With its strong ethic of equality, Norway should be able, in time, to incorporate its new citizens into a more diversified society. For now, it has integrated newcomers into its extensive system of health and social benefits.

Government and International Relations

Norway's King presides over weekly Friday meetings of the cabinet and signs all bills and cabinet decisions, but his power as head of state is more formal than real, although he may play a political role in times of crisis. All three kings since independence in 1905 have been respected for their quiet questioning and commentary during these meetings but have refrained from public statements of policy.

Until the rules were changed in 1990 permitting women to inherit the crown, the royal succession had been in the direct male line. After Crown Prince Haakon Magnus, born in 1973, the succession will pass to his first-born child, regardless of gender.

The Storting

Only the Storting can enact and repeal laws, amend the Constitution, impose taxes and fees, appropriate money for government expenses,

Nobel Peace Prize

Each fall since 1901 a five-person committee at the Nobel Institute in Oslo has announced the winner of the Nobel Peace Prize, given to "the person, or body, who has done the most or the best work for brotherhood among nations, for the abolition or reduction of standing armies, and for the holding and promotion of peace congresses." In his will of 1895 Alfred Nobel, the Swedish inventor of dynamite, stipulated that the scientific prizes and the prize for literature should be awarded by Swedish institutions, but that the decision concerning the peace prize be left to a committee appointed by the Norwegian Storting.

At his death Norway and Sweden were still in a union, but Nobel may have been acknowledging the fact that Norwegians had already been supporting the principle of international arbitration.

The committee is an independent body, and its members are not usually members of Parliament. They consider nominations (recently averaging about one hundred per year) from peace organizations, previous winners, and other groups. They may refrain from awarding the prize (this has happened nineteen times), give the prize to one person or institution, or award a joint prize. Some awards are controversial—including the 1990 award to Mikhail Gorbachev, which provoked another Norwegian group to award a People's Peace Prize to the Lithuanian President, Vytautas Landsbergis.

and keep a check on governmental agencies. It appoints the Nobel Peace Prize committee.

The 165 members are elected every fourth year as representatives of their counties and their political parties. Alternates are also elected, in case the member dies, is absent, or becomes a member of the cabinet.

The number of representatives from each of the nineteen counties (ranging from four to fifteen) depends not only on population but also on geographical location. Norwegians consider it fairer to give peripheral regions "overrepresentation" at the expense of central ones. The strong tradition of regional identity governs the seating arrangements, whereby the representatives are grouped by county rather than by party.

Though everyone is elected to the same Storting, the members divide themselves into two divisions for the consideration of a new law. Three quarters of the members belong to the Odelsting (heritage of the people assembly), where a bill is first considered. One quarter sit in the Lagting (law assembly), where it is considered a second time. Members may not abstain on a vote. To become law, a bill must be passed by both bodies in succession and signed by the King meeting with the cabinet.

Cabinet members may be requested to meet in Parliament to answer questions from the floor. Strict rules forbid heckling, shouting, or applause in this disciplined assembly.

Cabinet

Since 1905 the cabinet has consisted of the Prime Minister and a number of other ministers (currently eighteen), most of whom head a government department such as Foreign Affairs, the Environment, or Church and Cultural Affairs. A new department is the Ministry of Development Cooperation. Cabinet members cannot be members of Parliament, but they must answer to them, and often individuals rotate between the cabinet and the Parliament. Cabinet appointments must be approved by the Storting and usually reflect its political composition.

Coalition cabinets drawing on several political parties have been common recently.

The cabinet meets several times a week, and though the Prime Minister has considerable influence, his or her power is said to be less than that of an American president or a British or Canadian prime minister. An extensive bureaucracy has developed to assist cabinet policy-making and to carry out procedures. Bureaucrats do not change with political changes. These government agencies often formulate policies that are refined in the cabinet and then proposed to the Storting.

Political Parties

Norway has an array of political parties. The Labor Party has been the largest since 1927, with increasing opposition from the Conservatives, who are often allied with the Center Party (formerly the Farmer's Party) and the Christian Democrats. Some political analysts point to the parliamentary election of 1989 as the end of a long period of stability, although others go back to 1973 (after the surprise vote against the EEC) for the beginnings of major shifts in traditional voter loyalties, including the demise of the old Liberal Party.

Recently there has been a shift in favor of the two poles of the political spectrum: toward the Socialist Left Party, partly from those dissatisfied with Labor due to a rise in the unemployment rate; and toward the Party of Progress, partly from those dissatisfied with Norway's refugee policy, high taxation, and heavy investment in social welfare.

The shifts in voting patterns have made it increasingly difficult to form stable cabinets, since either the Conservatives or Labor must build cabinets through coalitions. Norwegians also influence the political process through participation in hundreds of associations, with

Parliamentary Elections: Number of Representatives by Party 1953–1989

Party	1953	1957	1961	1965	1969	1973	1977	1981	1985	1989
Total	150	150	150	150	150	155	155	155	157	165
Labor	77	78	74	68	74	62	76	66	71	63
Conservative	27	29	29	31	29	29	41	53	50	37
Center	14	15	16	18	20	21	12	11	12	11
Christian Democratic	14	12	15	13	14	20	22	15	16	14
Socialist Left	—	—	2	2	—	16	2	4	6	17
Party of Progress	—	—	—	—	—	4	—	4	2	22
Liberal	15	15	14	18	13	2	2	2	—	—
Communist	3	1	—	—	—	—	—	—	—	—
Other	—	—	—	—	—	1	—	—	—	1

Adapted from *Statistisk Årbok 1990 (Statistical Yearbook of Norway 1990)* Oslo: Statistisk Sentralbyrå, p. 387.

social, economic, political, and recreational focuses, all of which encourage activism.

Religion

The Norwegian Constitution in 1814 declared that the religion of the government—the Church of Norway—should be Evangelical Lutheran. Jews, monks, and Jesuits were not allowed into the country. The ban against Jews was repealed in 1851 and against monks in 1897, but not until 1956 was the prohibition against Jesuits deleted. The original ban reflects the influence of Lutheran ministers at the Eidsvoll Assembly.

In the past the Church of Norway has been active at a parish level in aiding the poor, and during World War II it was informally organized as an anti-Nazi front under the leadership of a Common Christian Council. During the war the churches were crowded, unlike today.

Currently about 85 percent of the Norwegian population are members of the Church of Norway, although only 2 or 3 percent attend church services. Religious instruction is given as part of the state school system unless parents specifically request that their children be exempted.

Among active members there is strong support for foreign missions as well as home mission and youth work. Per capita, Norway has more

The Tromsdalen Church, across the narrow sound from Tromsø, is also called the Arctic Cathedral. It stands as a "pyramid of lights" in the darkness of the arctic winter and is meant to symbolize Christ's return in glory. Ola Røe

Fridtjof Nansen

Fridtjof Nansen (1861–1930) led the Norwegian delegation in Geneva from the first League of Nations' session (in 1920) until his death and played a heroic role in the bitter decade after World War I. He took on the assignment of League of Nations High Commissioner for Prisoners of War and administered the repatriation of some 450,000 former prisoners of war.

He also took on the even heavier burden of bringing relief to the millions of refugees and displaced persons uprooted in Europe and Asia during the war. When refugees could not cross international borders because they lacked proper identification documents, Nansen introduced a new form of supranational passport, "the Nansen passport," which he persuaded more than fifty governments to recognize. He also persuaded them to accept quotas of refugees.

When Nansen was awarded the Nobel Peace Prize for his achievements in refugee relief in 1922, he was already in the midst of another assignment. At the request of the International Committee of the Red Cross, he personally led an immense famine-relief operation in the Soviet Union from 1921 to 1923. When the League did not support the project, he contributed the funds from his peace prize. Most diplomats said the task was impossible. Nansen started with tons of Norwegian cod-liver oil. He saved more than 7 million people, 6 million of them children, though he was deeply affected by the fact that thousands of others died.

Probably the greatest single achievement in Nansen's refugee work was the resettlement and exchange of several hundred thousand Greeks and Turks who fled to Greece following the defeat of the Greek Army in 1922 (see *The Land and People of Turkey*). This rescue operation took eight years to accomplish and involved building new villages and industries for the resettled Greeks and Turks. His last project was particularly difficult: trying to assist resettlement of Armenians.

The tradition of bringing aid to innocent victims of war, political up-heavals, natural catastrophes, and other disasters continues in Norway today.

Nansen tastes the food in a relief orphanage during a visit to Armenia on behalf of Armenian refugees. Norwegian Information Service, New York

The famous Nansen passport that he invented so that stateless persons might travel. Norwegian Information Service, New York

missionaries in Africa, Asia, and Latin America than any other country in the world. There continues to be a major split between the liberal and conservative branches of the church.

Today other religions have freedom to practice in Norway and receive state aid in proportion to their membership. The largest of these groups are the Pentecostalists, Lutheran Free Churches, Methodists, Roman Catholics, and Baptists. There are several thousand Muslims, and fewer than 1,000 Jews.

International Cooperation

Norway has a tradition of participating actively in international organizations that support peaceful cooperation. These have included the League of Nations, the United Nations, and the Nordic Council. Fridtjof Nansen was the League of Nations' High Commissioner for Prisoners of War; Trygve Lie (1896–1968) was the first United Nations Secretary-General (serving 1946–1953); and Gro Harlem Brundtland was chair of the World Commission on Environment and Development.

Since 1983 Norway has contributed at least a full 1 percent of its gross national product (GNP) to development aid, well above the average 0.35 percent contribution made by industrialized western countries and the UN's suggestion of 0.7 percent. Norway's own development aid is reviewed to make sure it improves the situation of women and that it supports "sustainable development"—that is, development that is not ecologically harmful and that follows the guidelines outlined by the World Commission on Environment and Development.

Norway is one of the four nations that keep a permanent force of soldiers ready for United Nations' peacekeeping missions and has contributed to all such missions. Since its founding in 1952 Norway has also been active in the Nordic Council, which seeks to coordinate cultural exchange, research, and social welfare benefits among Denmark, Finland, Iceland, Norway, and Sweden. The most significant result of the work carried out by the Nordic Council in the eyes of the average citizen is probably freedom to travel within the member countries without passports and the unified labor market that allows Nordic citizens to work and reside anywhere in the five countries without work or residence permits.

Holidays

"We use our holidays to celebrate the sun. We celebrate the arrival of the sun, the summer solstice, we journey to the mountains in search of the sun, and on the day we miss it most, because it is farthest away, we cheer ourselves with a grand Christmas feast," writes Thor Heyerdahl. Festivals in Norway really do follow the sun. Norway's most important festival—Constitution Day on May 17—celebrates Norway's independence, but the parades also highlight the coming of spring. Midsummer's Eve (June 23) marks the high point of the sun, Christmas candles create a bright environment in the midst of winter darkness, and Easter brings a reunion with the sun even though there is still snow on the ground.

May 17th: Constitution Day, Children's Day

The Norwegian equivalent of the American Fourth of July falls on May 17, the anniversary of the day in 1814 when Norway's popularly elected National Assembly issued a constitution that decreed an end to the country's four-century alliance with Denmark.

Constitution Day always falls on May 17, but it has been celebrated many different ways. Marching together behind one banner or in separate groups behind many, Norwegians show how they are feeling about their country and about political issues in their Constitution Day parades.

The first processions were united behind banners with the slogan "Guard the Constitution," because the Swedish King was trying to limit the powers given to the Storting in the Constitution. As the King's policies eased, the day took on a less defiant tone, and children joined the processions.

After complete independence in 1905 the parades emphasized nationhood. Commemorating Constitution Day was forbidden by the Nazi regime during World War II. The poet Nordahl Grieg (1902–1943), who died in action during the war, expressed most Norwegians' feelings about this prohibition:

> *Now stands the flagpole bare*
> *Behind Eidsvoll's budding trees.*
> *But in such an hour as this,*
> *We know what freedom is.*

Since World War II parades have stressed democratic rights, constitutional government, and freedom of the press.

There have been other times when Norwegians could not unite behind a single banner. During the 1870's and 1880's the day reflected political struggles between the two evolving political parties, the Conservatives (Høyre) and the Liberals (Venstre), and towns often had two parades and two sets of speakers. In the 1920's and 1930's many on the left boycotted the parade. One party leader said: "It is not in cooperation between the classes, but in the class struggle to the bitter end that the answer is to be found—on 17 May as on the other days of the year." In 1971 and 1972 supporters of membership in the European Economic Community and opponents marched separately and carried very different banners.

The Seventeenth of May has also become Norway's children's day. Thousands of schoolchildren parade with their school bands in every village, town, and city. Since 1905 the Oslo parade, which often includes over 60,000 children, has ended at the Royal Palace, where the royal family waves from the balcony. In 1983 a school in Oslo received a threat warning foreign students not to participate in the May 17 parade. In a show of support, the Norwegian children surrounded the newcomers and half the Storting marched with them.

The day is always a long one, with firecrackers set off at dawn (between 4 and 5 A.M.). High school seniors, wearing their red graduation hats and red jumpsuits, drive around town in cars decorated with flowers and branches. For them, Constitution Day begins a three-week celebration of the end of school.

Younger students and their parents wear new clothes with the national colors of red, blue, and white, or *bunad*s, the regional costumes that most Norwegians have for special occasions. Along with the parades there are memorial services at the tombs of national heroes, patriotic speeches, and brass bands. Everywhere the Norwegian flag is seen flying from flagpoles or being waved by hand.

Midsummer's Eve (June 23)

Midsummer is the longest day of the year. The feast of bonfires at the summer solstice is one of the oldest celebrations in northern Europe. Witches were said to meet on this day long ago, in special places, such as the high Domen hill near Vardø in the far north. Early Vikings often held their yearly *ting* then. In Christian times the holiday was renamed St. John's Eve, in honor of John the Baptist.

Huge heaps of wood—from twigs to tar barrels and fish crates—are collected for days along the shores of lakes, rivers, fjords, and the sea before they are set on fire on Midsummer's Eve and the crowd joins in dancing, eating, and drinking through the night.

May 17 is a holiday for everyone—young or old.   The Royal Norwegian Ministry of Foreign Affairs, Oslo

Everyone hopes that the summer will be long, though there is always the fear that just as it is beginning it is also ending, and one must catch every midsummer moment. All too soon it will be All Saints' Day (November 1) and the beginning of *mørketiden* ("the murky time"), a particularly dreary time of darkness and cloudiness before the snows add lightness and the skiing season begins.

Jul (Christmas)

By November Norwegians start to count the days until Christmas. It is a busy season for churches with special Advent services, for stores that experience their busiest time, and for housework. Traditionally, all the wood must be cut, cakes baked, food prepared, and Yule beer brewed by St. Thomas's Day, December 21.

Though the original meanings are debated and many details forgotten, most Christmas traditions have long histories connected with early northern European efforts to appease ghosts and to encourage a good agricultural year. The Christmas tree and St. Nicholas (or Santa Claus) are recent arrivals from Germany and the United States but have been enthusiastically incorporated into this lengthy holiday. Even before the Christmas tree came indoors, sailors tied a tree on the mast of every ship sailing under a Norwegian flag.

Banquet of the Ghosts

Before St. Nicholas or Santa Claus were imported into department stores, Christmastime was associated with ghosts. Norwegians believed that ancestors returned to their earthly homes in midwinter. Until the late nineteenth century, in some districts, straw was left for the "invisible guests" to sleep on through the holidays, and a few loaves of bread were set out on the kitchen table for them to eat. A favorite Norwegian

The Special Ghost of Christmas

Each farm had a special ghost named *Haugkallen* or "the old man of the mound," who was believed to be the ghost of the first settler of that farm. He had brought the lands under cultivation and stayed as the protector of the farm as long as the current residents were on good terms with him. At Christmastime he had to have a bowl of porridge delivered to his headquarters in the barn.

The image of this much-respected and -feared ghost has gradually changed into a fairy-tale-like character. Called a *nisse*, a form of the name Nicholas, he is now rather like one of Santa's elves. Today the newer *julemannen* ("Christmas man"), like our Santa Claus, is sometimes also called *nisse* and in some families brings the gifts to the door. There are still families where a bowl of porridge is delivered to the barn for tradition's sake.

fairy tale, "The Cat of Dovre," tells of a family that regularly fled its house to make room for an invading horde of Yule ghosts. The ghosts, or trolls in some versions, were finally outwitted one year by a white bear, the "cat" in the title, and never returned again.

In the eighteenth century food was often left on the table day and night from Christmas Eve to Epiphany (January 6), and all who entered the house had to have a bite to eat, for if they left without eating it was said they would "carry Christmas out of the house." Today Christmas hospitality still includes a special porridge for the *nisse*, food for birds, and a meal for all the farm animals on Christmas Eve. The birds eat from a *julenek*, a sheaf of oats put on a pole. In the past this was considered a magical way to keep the birds from damaging the following year's crops.

The Twenty Days of Christmas

After a traditional Christmas Eve meal the family goes into the living room and walks around the Christmas tree singing carols. The tree is decorated with white candles, which folklorists see as a trace of the traditional midwinter bonfires. Church services, held on Christmas Eve, Christmas Day, and New Year's Eve, act as a transition from the family to community celebrations that continue for many days with rounds of visiting and exchanges of gifts.

"Twentieth-day Knut drives the Yule out" is an old expression referring to the housecleaning (driving out the ghosts?) at the end of Christmas. The twenty days of Christmas extend from December 25 to January 13, St. Knut's Day.

Easter

Easter does not mark the arrival of spring—it's still too early for that—but the lengthening of the day. The Sami gather in Karasjok to celebrate weddings, confirmation, baptism, and the end of the long polar night. Many Norwegians set off on skis for a solitary journey to commune with nature. Others find a spot on a plateau to sunbathe, leaning against a cabin surrounded by snow. In the mountains the first weak rays of spring sun are intensified as they reflect off the blazing snow.

"Like lemmings heading the wrong way, Norwegians drive up into the mountains . . . and disappear into the vast landscapes where nobody lives" is how Norwegian journalist Bjørn Lindahl described the Easter exodus in 1990. Extra trains leave the cities, and Norway's state radio broadcasts warnings to people not to push themselves too hard— "Don't be ashamed to turn back"—as Norwegians take a five-day break from school and work. Movie theaters and most restaurants close, and even garbage collection is suspended for a week.

Some Norwegians stretch the holiday by taking regular vacation days in addition to the Easter days in order to immerse themselves in the sun. Though many spend the time with family and very close friends, Easter is also a celebration of solitude and of independence. An oft-told story concerns a Norwegian professor who was asked how he had enjoyed his mountain holiday. "It was a total failure," he replied. "I met somebody."

Other Holidays

May 1—May Day—is Labor Day. In recent years more workers have spent the day getting their summer cabins or boats ready than marching in parades. But Labor Day has, as it does throughout Europe, a long tradition associated with unions and the Labor Party. It is the time to demand a shorter work week, better working conditions, better retirement benefits, or whatever is the primary issue of that year. "Unity is strength" is a frequently heard slogan, and each year there are specific demands as well. But many feel there is little left to demand in Norway, where everyone is entitled to four weeks' paid vacation (five weeks in some positions and after age sixty), two and a half days at Christmas, and a minimum of five days at Easter, with the additional holidays of Ascension Day, Whitsuntide Monday, May 1, and Constitution Day, not to mention sick days for oneself or to care for one's children. On Labor Day 1991 there were banners against Norway joining the EC, a debate which will continue for some time.

Various towns and regions have special events throughout the year. When the coastal steamer first set sail for year-round service on July 2, 1893, its arrival was celebrated as a national holiday all the way up the coast. For many years July 2 was referred to as the national day of North Norway. Others claim that Holmenkollen Sunday, when the ski-jumping contest is held on the slopes overlooking Oslo as part of the

Holmenkollen Ski Festival, represents Norway's second national day. Musical events take place throughout the summer. Bergen holds its concert and theater festival at the end of May (because this is when it is least likely to rain!). There is an international jazz week in Molde in July. The National Theater in Oslo has begun to hold an international Ibsen festival in the early fall, with performances by Norwegian acting companies and others from around the world. The Norwegian event that attracts the most international attention is the annual presentation of the Nobel Peace Prize, which takes place in Oslo every December 10.

Literature, Art, and Music

Literature

In 1814 no one could have predicted that Norway would become known through its creative artists. There were no great concert halls, no national theaters, and few public libraries.

Aside from the Old Norse saga literature of the thirteenth century and folk art, Norwegians had only the Bergen-born Ludvig Holberg (1684–1754) of the previous century to look back to. Holberg wrote brilliant comedies, essays, and satires, but he spent his whole writing life in Denmark and was treated as a Dane. In 1899, when the National Theater in Oslo opened, Ibsen sat in the front row, and Norway had produced many creative artists in the eighty-five years since Eidsvoll.

While they gave Norway a new cultural heritage, many painters, musicians, and writers felt the need to spend long periods abroad, since the country was at first still too narrow-minded to appreciate them. They went to the large European cultural centers in Italy, France, and Germany to renew themselves, while they continued to focus on Norwegian issues and themes in their work. These modern artists were responding to tensions within Norway as a rural culture met the modern world.

Poetry and Radical Politics: Henrik Wergeland

The first important writer of the modern period was Henrik Wergeland (1808–1845), who is sometimes called Norway's Shelley. He was a fiery and intense figure who plunged into contemporary events with passion and called upon his compatriots to free themselves of Danish influence.

Wergeland is considered Norway's greatest lyric poet. He wrote beautiful love and nature poems, in which he called clouds "wonderlands of the sun," a long epic poem, plays, and numerous essays. He also issued radical pamphlets, wrote a series of books of popular instruction (*For the Common People*, 1830–1839), and a periodical (*For the Working Class*, 1839–1845). He established a free personal lending library and a school in his own home, where he taught Norwegian and geography. In his short lifetime—he died at thirty-seven—he produced an entire literature and set the pattern for creative writers to be public advocates for democracy and freedom.

Wergeland lobbied for more than ten years to remove the article in the Constitution that banned Jews from Norway. In gratitude, the Jewish communities of Denmark and Sweden commissioned a statue in his honor, which now stands in Oslo but was first unveiled in 1847 in

Stockholm because the contributors, being Jewish, could not enter Norway.

Wergeland's sister, Camilla Collett (1813–1895), an advocate of women's emancipation, wrote Norway's first feminist novel, *The Governor's Daughter* (1855), based partly on her own life, decrying the position of women forced into marriage. She had loved her brother's enemy, Johan Welhaven (1807–1873), another gifted poet who was pro-Danish. The antagonism between the anti- and pro-Danish followers of Wergeland and Welhaven led to wild exchanges in the newspapers and sometimes to street fights in the 1830's and 1840's.

Collett's critical and realistic view of society inspired other writers later in the century. Amalie Skram (1846–1905) continued the tradition of female writers in her depiction of a series of disastrous marriages in novels such as *Constance Ring* (1885) and *Betrayed* (1892). Her frank description of the inner life of the women characters shocked many readers at the time.

"Now Is the Time . . ."

Starting in the 1850's Bjørnstjerne Bjørnson (1832–1910), the author of Norway's national anthem, followed in Wergeland's tradition. Bjørnson received the Nobel Prize for Literature in 1903, whereas Ibsen never did, a fact that shocks people today. Yet his contemporaries believed Bjørnson deserved the award. He was a well-known figure in European politics, fighting for the rights of minorities such as the Finns, Poles, and Slovaks, and for disarmament and peace.

Bjørnson was a person of tremendous energy, and even his friends sometimes sighed, "If only he'd stick to writing!" In 1905, when Norway was struggling to dissolve the union with Sweden (see Chapter X), Bjørnson sent a telegram to the Norwegian Prime Minister: "Now is the time to keep our front united." The Prime Minister replied: "Now is the time to keep our mouths shut."

In his long lifetime Bjørnson's many literary works of many different kinds—saga plays based on Norway's medieval history; poems; peasant tales; and realistic "problem" plays, which he introduced to Scandinavia—gave Norwegians confidence in their cultural heritage.

The Modern Breakthrough

Scandinavian critics call the period of the 1870's and 1880's, when writers began to deal realistically with burning social issues, "the modern breakthrough." This "new literature" was very apparent in Norway. For the first time Norwegian literature became the leader in Scandinavia, and Norwegian authors became known abroad as never before. At the top of the list was a writer of genius, the playwright Henrik Ibsen.

"Fighting in Heart and Brain with Trolls"

Ibsen is recognized worldwide as the founder of modern drama. His work revolutionized the theater. A supporter of women's rights, he is known for creating many great female characters. Ibsen's plays were so compelling that the young James Joyce taught himself Norwegian to be able to study them. The American actress Eva Le Gallienne (1899–1991), who translated and acted in many of his plays, exclaimed, "I would rather play Ibsen than eat."

Ibsen's major plays are set in Norway, and the landscape of fjords and seas and mountain avalanches is always present, but the characters and themes have universal significance. In the 1950's a Japanese critic saw *Peer Gynt* (1867), which is considered the most "Norwegian" of Ibsen's plays. He found that the boastful Peer, who refuses to make any commitments and always takes the "way around," was a recognizable Japanese type!

Ibsen's plays aroused enormous controversy, but people flocked to see them. In his realistic plays of the 1870's and 1880's he showed people as they are, struggling with all the problems society was afraid to mention: marital discord, bankruptcy, illegitimacy. A succession of plays scandalized the whole of Europe. *Pillars of Society* (1877), about a businessman who betrays love for money, was followed by *A Doll's House* (1879), perhaps Ibsen's best known play in America, about women's liberation and the hypocrisy of marriage. When Nora left her husband and children in the last scene, freeing herself of the childish role she had played as the dutiful wife, the shattering sound of the slamming door reverberated throughout the world, and it still does today.

Ghosts (1881) dealt with the lies surrounding sexually transmitted disease and all the "old dead opinions and all sorts of old dead beliefs and the like" that prevented people from developing and becoming fully themselves. It caused as great an uproar as *A Doll's House*. Ibsen was denounced by some critics as "a crazy, cranky being."

In *An Enemy of the People* (1882) he wrote the first modern ecology play, focusing on the way a small town hides the fact that its thermal baths, which are the source of its prosperity, are polluted. The hero, Dr. Stockmann, reveals the health hazard and is run out of town.

Ibsen's later plays acquired an even greater depth and complexity, as he probed the struggle of individuals to find the truth about themselves and lead fully human lives—to defeat the trolls within—in such works as *The Wild Duck* (1884), *Hedda Gabler* (1890), *The Master Builder* (1892), and *John Gabriel Borkman* (1896).

Over the course of fifty years, Ibsen published twenty-five plays and a volume of poetry. His works are still read and produced throughout the world.

Ibsen's Early Struggles

During the last half of his life Ibsen seemed able to produce a world-wide success every other year. It did not start out that way. At fifteen he was apprenticed to a pharmacist in the tiny village of Grimstad, south of Skien, where he was born. The work in a little dark room, smelling of chemicals and the open fire, was long and dreary. Ibsen was so poor, he could not afford socks or an overcoat. His first play, *Catilina* (1850), was printed in 300 copies, of which only thirty were sold. He sold the rest for wrapping paper one day when he was penniless. When Ibsen became famous, he dressed well.

Ibsen spent a dozen years learning the craft of theater inside and out, as Molière and Shakespeare had, as stage manager of the new theaters in Bergen (1851–1857) and Oslo (1857–1862), established to promote Norwegian plays and actors. But his own work won little recognition, and he was blamed when the theater in Oslo went bankrupt in 1862. He applied over and over again for grants and was turned down.

At age thirty-six, finally collecting a small scholarship but in great despair, Ibsen left Norway in 1864. He lived in Italy and Germany for twenty-seven years before he returned permanently to his homeland.

Twentieth-Century Nobel Laureates

In the 1890's Knut Hamsun (1859–1952) called for a new kind of literature that would deal with "the whisper of the blood . . . and all the unconscious life of the mind." Before Sigmund Freud's psychological theories were internationally accepted, Hamsun described the hidden

Ibsen said he wrote "to make people think." At the end of his life, residents of Oslo could set their watches by Ibsen's daily walk—dressed in top hat and cloak—along Karl Johansgate to the Grand Hotel, where he had his own special table and chair in the cafe.
Norwegian Information Service, New York

internal workings of the mind in a series of innovative novels. His early novels—*Hunger* (1890), about a starving writer, *Mysteries* (1892), and *Pan* (1894)—explored the irrational and mysterious aspects of the individual psyche and immediately established him as one of the most important writers in Europe. He was especially popular in Germany and the Soviet Union and had a major influence on many twentieth-century authors, including the American Henry Miller. In 1920 he was awarded the Nobel Prize for Literature.

Hamsun was critical of many trends in modern life, and his views were politically reactionary. He supported Germany during World War I and again in World War II; the latter is much harder for Norwegians to forgive. During the occupation of Norway by Germany, Hamsun was a member of the Norwegian Nazi party, the Nasjonal Samling.

A few weeks after the invasion, on May 4, 1940, he wrote an article in the Nazi newspaper *Fritt Folk* (*Free People*) ridiculing King Haakon, whom he called the "runaway King," and the Norwegians' attempts to mobilize: "It is to no avail that each one of you has grabbed his gun and stands frothing at the Germans; tomorrow or the next day you will be bombed."

When Norway was liberated, Hamsun was an old man of eighty-five. Collaborators were brought to trial in the summer of 1945. Hamsun was examined by a group of psychiatrists, who declared him to be "of impaired mental capacity," and he was given a very heavy fine, almost his entire net worth, but he was not imprisoned. He wrote his last novel, *On Overgrown Paths* (1949), when he was eighty-nine to prove that he was sane.

Hamsun causes great conflicts for Norwegians. On the one hand, they recognize that he is a great writer. After Ibsen, he is the greatest writer Norway has produced. On the other hand, his Nazism goes against their deepest traditions.

Sigrid Undset

Sigrid Undset (1882-1949), Norway's greatest woman writer, offers a sharp contrast to Hamsun. She received the Nobel Prize in 1928 for her long historical novel *Kristin Lavransdatter* (1920–1922), set in thirteenth-century Norway, which tells the story of Kristin from her childhood to old age. Undset's father was a well-known archaeologist whose specialty was the Iron Age in Europe. From an early age she was aware of Old Norse sagas and Scandinavian folk songs.

Historians praise her accuracy and knowledge, but her historical novels became international best-sellers because she was a great story-teller and a perceptive psychologist. In addition to the novels about the Middle Ages, Undset also wrote many essays and realistic novels set in contemporary Oslo. In all, she published thirty-six books.

Today there is renewed interest in her work in Norway. Although she is not regarded as a feminist, her novels provide insights into women's lives that are not found elsewhere in Norwegian fiction. Her early novels, such as *Jenny* (1911), center on the lives of ordinary working women and the conflict between personal ambition and the demands of family life. She gave up her own plans to be a painter after the death of her father and worked as a secretary for ten years supporting her mother and two younger sisters. She later raised five children with little help from their father.

In 1925 Undset converted to Catholicism, and in the 1930's she wrote extensively against the rise of Nazism in Germany and Communism in the Soviet Union. There are still a few people in North Norway who remember seeing an older woman in 1940 trudging along on skis and collapsing, exhausted, in a snowdrift. Undset was fleeing the invading Germans, who had her on a list of people who were to be arrested. The writer's escape to Sweden, across Siberia, then to Japan, and finally to the United States, which she reached in August 1940, is recounted in *Return to the Future* (1942).

Undset spent the wars years in Brooklyn, New York, and was a tireless worker for the Norwegian government-in-exile, giving lectures, writing articles and radio shows. She made friends with Americans—particularly Dorothy Day, who was running a settlement for jobless youngsters in Manhattan, and the novelist Willa Cather. At the end of the war she returned to her home in Lillehammer. Worn out from the war, she did not begin any other major works. She died quietly in her sleep four years later. The Norwegian government awarded her the highest decorations for her literary and patriotic contributions.

As Norway approaches the twenty-first century, its writers are drawn on the one hand into a very international world of social and political issues, and on the other into a very internal world of personal issues. Some writers continue the trend of regionalism, focusing on their particular place of birth, often in local dialect. It is difficult to generalize amidst the diversity, except to point out that—perhaps because Norway is a very tightly knit country—there is renewed interest in personal memoirs and biographies of Norwegians. A 1985 example is the unusual life story of the current president of the Storting, Jo Benkow, *Fra Synagogen til Løvebakken* (*From the Synagogue to the Lion's Hill*).

Art and Music

Edvard Munch: Dissecting Souls

Edvard Munch's (1863–1944) ability to portray the trauma of modern psychic life through intense distortion of colors and forms made him one of the most powerful and influential of modern artists. Many of

Norwegians have been carving for over 3,000 years, including rock carvings (a), Viking furnishings (b), eighteenth century folk art (c), and twentieth-century boxes (d). The Norwegian Information Service, New York

these early paintings were also transformed into etchings, lithographs, or woodcuts by Munch—art media in which his approach was considered revolutionary.

Munch came from an old Norwegian professional family. His father's brother, Peter Andreas Munch, was one of the leading historians of his age. However, Edvard's earliest years were overshadowed by the untimely deaths of his mother (when he was just five) and his eldest sister (when he was fourteen), his own illness, and a highly religious and overbearing father. Many critics look to Munch's childhood to explain the melancholy expressed in his paintings. Munch's views on the human condition were also influenced by Hans Jaeger (1854–1910) and his circle of radical anarchists, whom Munch met in 1889. That year Munch wrote: "No one should paint interiors anymore, people reading and women knitting. They should be living people who breathe and feel, suffer and love."

In the 1890's much of his effort went into an ambitious series of pictures that he called *Frieze of Life: A Poem of Life, Love and Death*. Munch's first exhibition in Berlin in 1892 had to be closed due to the public uproar. Munch commented, "Just as Leonardo da Vinci studied human anatomy and dissected corpses, so I try to dissect souls."

During his early period Munch spent much time in France and Germany, but he, like many landscape artists before him, usually returned to Norway in the summer. After spending the winter of 1908–1909 in a clinic in Copenhagen to rest his nerves and to give up smoking and drinking, he returned to live in Norway until his death in 1944. Munch's later work reflects more harmony and simplicity, including

Christian Krogh (1852–1925) was the first director of the Art Academy in Oslo, founded in 1909, and influenced younger painters, including Edvard Munch and his son Per Krogh (1889–1965), known for his murals in many public buildings, including the U.N. in New York. Norwegian Information Service, New York

winter scenes from the Oslo Fjord and other landscapes, a number of pictures of workers, portraits, and a series of self-portraits.

Munch gave his works to the city of Oslo, where they are now housed at the Munch Museum, opened in 1963. Artists from around the world come to look at the paintings of one of the great Expressionists and to study his techniques first hand.

Edvard Grieg: The Sound of Norway

Norwegian music has long built on rural traditions that include folk songs, the playing of the fiddle, and brass bands. Almost every grade school has a marching brass band, as do many towns. Many of Norway's jazz musicians had their start in these brass bands. The orchestra tradition was much slower to develop, and only in the 1990's was Oslo's Philharmonic Orchestra increased to the international standard of 110 players.

Norway's greatest composer is Edvard Hagerup Grieg (1843–1907), in whose works Norwegians hear cascading waterfalls, wild mountains, milkmaids' tunes, and Hardanger fiddlers, though always with new harmonies.

Grieg did not write symphonies (one composed in his youth has the instructions, "must never be performed" written in his handwriting), but he took on large projects, such as writing the music for Ibsen's *Peer Gynt*; this "incidental music" achieved fame all over the world. The Piano Concerto in A minor, Opus 16 ranks highest of all Grieg's orchestral compositions, but he is also known for his piano sonata and

In Skrik (The Cry *or* The Scream) *Munch personified a general sense of anxiety, which he called "a scream against nature." His use of space and color is seen as a break-through in modern art by many scholars. Here the sky is a mix of intense oranges, reds, and yellows, though the work is also often reprinted in its black-and-white lithograph format.* Norwegian Information Service, New York

ten volumes of lyrical pieces, inspired by poems by Bjørnson, Ibsen, Arne Garborg (1851–1924), as well as Norwegian folk poems.

Grieg was born and died in Bergen, to which his paternal grandfather had emigrated from Aberdeen, Scotland, in 1779. He built a home, Trollhaugen ("The Hill of the Trolls"), on a wooded lakeside outside Bergen. Since 1953 Bergen has held its annual music festival there. As the 150th anniversary of his birth (1993) approached, musicologists noted that a new generation of musicians is rediscovering the range of Grieg's work, including stage music, chamber music, and many of his songs, which with one or two exceptions are little known outside Scandinavia.

Arne Nordheim

For almost two generations after the death of Grieg, Norwegians did not seem ready for even minor musical revolutions. Arne Nordheim (born 1931) represents major change. Since the 1950's he has written experimental works, often combining orchestral music with taped electronically processed acoustic sounds. His music is heard in unusual contexts, such as in and around a "sound sculpture" that he and sculptor Arnold Haukeland created for the blind. On one day, in six different cities, Nordheim created a music event that combined children's choirs, symphony orchestras, church-bell players, an ancient music ensemble, a Hardanger fiddle player, a Morse code tapper, reciters, and tape.

Sports and Exploration

Norwegians have been skiing for at least four thousand years and possibly longer. A rock carving in Nordland near the Arctic Circle shows a person on two skis. Skis about 2,000 years old have been found preserved in bogs. The importance of skis for hunting, visiting, or even spying on enemies, is reflected in Old Norse mythology, which had both a ski god (Ull) and a ski goddess (Skade).

Sondre Norheim: Founder of Modern Skiing

Though skis and snowshoes were probably common throughout the circumpolar area, Norway takes credit as the home of modern skiing as a sport. Sondre Norheim (1825–1897), a poor tenant farmer and maker of weavers' shuttles in Morgedal, in Telemark, ended a 4,000-year tradition by devising a "waisted" ski (narrower in the middle), called the Telemark ski, and using stiff ski bindings around the heel. These enabled him to swing and to jump at his reckless pace without having his skis fall off.

Norheim is also credited with the idea of skiing as a sport—to some people's concern that he was not properly caring for his large family. He did not always finish his shuttle orders. One winter he dug up the seed potatoes he had been given by the poor-law authorities and ate them one by one for dinner. When he ran out of wood, Norheim carved chips off the barn wall.

"They Must Be Mad"

Norheim amazed his neighbors in the valley with his feats of fast skiing and jumping (legend says that he often went over the roofs of barns) and led parishioners on ski trips after church services many Sundays. A tireless teacher, Norheim and a group of men from Morgedal became known throughout the country. At first they had to ski to a competition even if it was a hundred miles away, but soon Norheim and a few others had their trips and lodging paid for so they could demonstrate their techniques. A Danish prince, one of the spectators in 1879 in Christiania, as Oslo was then called, watched the first man from Telemark soar out from a jump with a little branch in one hand while he took off his cap with the other. The prince is said to have exclaimed, "This can't be true! They must be mad."

By the time Norheim was fifty, his legs became stiffer. He retired from competitions but helped the children of Morgedal until, at age fifty-nine, he followed his son to America where skiing had already been introduced by others from Telemark.

Just before the turn of the century, Norwegians studying engineering

The Huseby ski jumping contest in Oslo in 1879 initiated the famous Holmenkollen competitions, which today draw up to 100,000 spectators. Norwegian Tourist Board, New York

and architecture in Germany and Switzerland shocked residents in Chamonix in the French Alps by using an old barn as an improvised ski jump. Hotels that had previously closed in the winter discovered a new type of vacation, and in 1924 the first Winter Olympics were held in Chamonix, with Norwegians taking the first four places in the 30-mi. (50-km.) race.

The first recorded skiing competition with prizes in Norway dates from 1866. The history of the Holmenkollen sky-high ski jump outside Oslo goes back to 1892. By 1903 foreigners joined in the annual competitions. Norwegians do not grow up thinking of skiing as a competition—it is simply the national passion. This need not prevent them from being champions as when they triumphed in cross-country and Alpine skiing in the Winter Olympic Games of 1992.

At age two or three Norwegians make their first unsteady trips on skis; in school they look forward to ski days and ski vacations, and as adults they often take off on skis to unwind after a day at work, skiing the many miles of lighted trails or through the woods wearing a light on a cap. Norwegians even ski in the summer on the glaciers in Jotunheimen National Park.

It has been said that if you want to judge the wealth of Norwegians, you must look at their cars or boats but not their skis. Everyone invests in an equally good pair now that Norway has one of the highest standards of living in the world.

Ice Skating Heroes

Years ago ice skating was more popular than it is now, and it required a smaller investment in equipment. The first great speed-skating contest in Norway was held on the fjord near Oslo's fortress of Akershus in 1885, and speed-skating champions were national heroes through the early 1950's. Norway got a new national hero in February 1991, when Johan Koss made sports history by breaking three world records during the world speed-skating championships in the Netherlands, followed by winning a gold medal at the 1992 Winter Olympics.

The 1930's saw Sonja Henie bring fame to Norway as the world's figure-skating champion at thirteen—a title she kept for ten years—and an Olympic gold medalist three times. She emigrated to Hollywood to become a film star, but returned to build a major modern art collection, which she and her husband donated to the city of Oslo.

Norway's most popular group sport is soccer.   Ola Røe

Sports for the Handicapped

Races of an entirely different type began with the Ridderrennet (Ski for Light) started in 1964 by Erling Stordahl, himself blind, who arranged the first ski race for the visually handicapped with deeper trails and a system of beeping sounds along the track. His initiative was followed by others, and the disabled of many categories now enjoy their own events in seventeen different sports organized by the Norwegian Sports Organization for the Disabled, founded in 1971. It is part of the Norwegian Sports Federation, Norway's largest organization with over a million members, funded by a state-run soccer betting pool.

Marathons for Women

Norwegian women today are carrying off many top trophies in international sports as marathon runners and cross-country skiers, and in women's handball and soccer teams. But their participation in sports was not accepted immediately. When skiing began as a leisure activity, Norwegian women and girls in the countryside often joined in, and in 1888 Lillehammer sponsored the world's first ski races for women. However, men in Oslo were very critical of women skiers daring to drink a mug of beer or to stretch their legs by a fireplace to warm up after skiing. Only since the 1960's have Norwegian women been taken seriously in cross-country competitions.

The acceptance of Norwegian women as athletes is often attributed to the barriers broken by Grete Waitz (b. 1953) as a marathon runner. She won the New York marathon nine times out of ten between 1978 and 1988 and started a run for women through the streets of Oslo in 1982. It has become an annual event in which her own mother participates.

Though sports are an integral part of Norwegian life, in case any Norwegians manage not to be athletic, the government launched a campaign in 1990 called "People in Shape for the Olympics" to be sure that everyone is involved in some kind of physical activity by 1994.

Exploits on Skis

Just as skis and boats are part of Norway's main sports, their use and an honest respect for nature are the keys to the Norwegian contribution to exploration, which has included a host of people from the Viking adventurers to Fridtjof Nansen, Otto Sverdrup, Roald Amundsen, and Thor Heyerdahl.

Norwegian Ski Terms

Skiers may not realize how much Norwegian they know.

1. *Ski* (pronounced "shee" in Norwegian)—a piece of wood.
2. *Slalåm* or *slalom*—from the Telemark dialect and from Old Norse. *Sla* means a smooth and slanting hill or slope, and *lom* means a trail or track. Today, slalom indicates a steep trail or downhill skiing race in a winding course.
3. Telemark—the name of a method by which a skier terminates a downhill run by making an elegant turn and then braking; the term comes from the region in Norway where this method was perfected by the farmers of Morgedal between 1860 and 1880.
4. Christiania or just Christie—a turn executed by parallel skis. Telemarkers claim it originated in Telemark and was misnamed when it was instituted into the skiing curriculum in 1901 in Christiania, the capital of Norway, renamed Oslo in 1925.

Nansen's daring 1888 month-long trip on skis across the Greenland ice cap where others had previously tried and turned back, called the world's attention to skiing. It also provided training for Nansen's best-known exploit, his journey across the Arctic Ocean with the polar ship *Fram* in 1893–1896.

Nansen's Polar Expedition

Nansen was not a crazy person with "illogical schemes of self-destruction," as some skeptics thought, but a serious scientist who hypothesized that the Arctic current flowed from Siberia toward the North Pole and from there down to Greenland. His theory was based on some samples of driftwood found off Greenland that could be traced to Siberian trees, among other evidence. To test his hypothesis, Nansen designed a special boat that would drift and not break apart under the enormous pressure of the ice pack. He took enough food for six years, fuel oil for eight years, and a hand-picked crew of thirteen people who he thought could withstand monotony without going mad or resorting to violence.

After heading east in July 1893, the *Fram* entered the ice off the northeast coast of Siberia and was frozen into the ice pack, as planned. The boat zigzagged across the polar sea as the crew grew fat "like prize pigs," and Nansen felt almost ashamed of the easy life in spite of the hours spent in scientific study—taking soundings and temperatures and recording magnetic observations.

After almost two years Nansen realized the boat would not pass over the North Pole, though his drift theory was basically correct and the *Fram* reached a record north latitude. This gave Nansen the excuse he needed to set off toward the North Pole by land.

With only one companion, Hjalmar Johansen, three light sleds, twenty-eight dogs, three kayaks, and food for one hundred days, Nansen set out on March 14, 1895, to struggle north from the icebound ship. By early April he recognized that he couldn't reach the North Pole, though he had gone farther than any previous explorer. Then the question was making it back to Franz Joseph Land, 400 mi. (640 km.) to the southwest. (Franz Joseph Land is a group of islands north of Siberia and east of Svalbard.) By the time he reached an uninhabited island north of Franz Joseph Land, it was August and winter was closing in. Nansen and Johansen dug a three-foot hollow in the ground, made a roof of walrus skins, and sat out the long nine-month winter.

There were plenty of walruses and polar bears to eat, although the monotony was maddening.

On June 17, 1896, Nansen made it to one of the southern islands when he thought he heard a dog barking. The dog belonged to an English explorer, Frederick Jackson, who, ironically, had been commissioned to seek a land route to the North Pole just as Nansen had been proving that the North Pole was surrounded by frozen ocean. Nansen returned to Norway on Jackson's ship to a hero's welcome. The *Fram*, meanwhile, had drifted from Siberia to Svalbard, proving Nansen right. It arrived back in Norway a week after he did. Nansen's victory symbolized to the Norwegians their desire to succeed even against the greatest odds—a desire that, on the national level, was focused on gaining total independence from Sweden.

Otto Sverdrup

Otto Sverdrup (1854–1930) was captain of the *Fram* for Nansen's drift and had also taken part in Nansen's earlier Greenland expedition. In his own right he was a dedicated explorer. He took the *Fram* on a second voyage to the Arctic islands north of Canada and spent four years (1898–1902) charting 100,000 sq. mi. (260,000 sq. km.) of unexplored territory, later leading other polar expeditions between 1910 and 1920. His maps opened a new world to other explorers.

Crossing the Northwest Passage

The Arctic attracted a number of amateur explorers, but Roald Amundsen (1872–1928), like Nansen, was a professional. He read and analyzed the works of all explorers and decided that success meant combining the role of scientist and navigator. He not only hardened himself physically, playing soccer and skiing and sleeping with his bedroom window open in the winter, but studied navigation and science, particularly the field of magnetism.

Amundsen's dream was to become the first person to navigate the Northwest Passage. In the previous four hundred years, fifty or sixty expeditions had tried, and all had had to give up. In 1903 he set out on a small herring boat that was thirty-one years old, with a crew of six. He believed that smallness and patience would go farther than large vessels and force.

Amundsen got through the entire Northwest Passage, including a shallow, island-dotted strait never previously navigated. "It was just like sailing through an uncleared field," he wrote later. Other boats had been too big and awkward to succeed.

During the voyage Amundsen spent one summer and two winters

Though he was sometimes away for months or even years, Roald Amundsen enjoyed returning home to "Svartskog" (Black Forest) near Oslo. Norwegian Infomation Service, New York

doing research on King William Island surrounded by Netsilik Inuit (Eskimos). He and his crew wore Inuit-style clothing and slept in snow houses. British explorers wore wool, which sometimes created frozen sweat, while the Norwegians were comfortable in deerskin underwear and boots stuffed with sedge grass.

Amundsen attributed part of his success to the lesson of patience he (and Nansen earlier) learned from the Inuit. Earlier explorers had often called the native people lazy, when the issue was really a matter of proper pacing. The Inuit knew that sweat can kill you in the Arctic and that you must never be so tired that you can't get an extra burst of energy in an emergency. Amundsen left the Inuit with the feeling that their way of life had more integrity than what was called "civilization," a theme that Thor Heyerdahl was to pick up on in the Pacific thirty years later.

Reaching the South Pole

In September 1909, just as Amundsen was planning to go to the North Pole in the trustworthy *Fram*, the world heard that the American Robert Peary had reached it. Amundsen quickly changed his course—without telling his crew at first—and headed for Antarctica. He would try to beat Robert Scott's British expedition to the South Pole.

At the Bay of Whales in the Ross Sea, Amundsen set out with four men and fifty-two dogs on the expedition that made his name known the world over. One of the four men was Olav Bjaaland, a skiing champion from Morgedal, who was chosen to make sure the skis and sleds would be in top condition all the time. On December 14, 1911, the Norwegians reached the South Pole and planted the Norwegian flag on King Haakon VII's Plateau.

Amundsen died in 1928 trying to rescue another explorer, Umberto

Amundsen and his companions reached the South Pole five weeks before Scott and his exhausted men arrived to find the Norwegian flag and Amundsen's tent. Norwegian Information Service, New York

Nobile, whose airship had crashed during an attempt to fly over the North Pole. Nansen said at his memorial service that Amundsen thus "returned to the expanses of the Arctic Ocean, where his life's work lay."

Thor Heyerdahl: Navigation as Cultural Contact

The most widely known Norwegian explorer of contemporary times, Thor Heyerdahl (b. 1914), has not focused on the polar regions or, strictly speaking, on unknown territories. But he has challenged established theories of archaeology by listening to the local people in various cultures and studying navigation.

At the university Heyerdahl studied zoology and geography. His first trip to Polynesia in 1937 was as a student to do research on animal life in the valleys of the small island of Fatu-Hiva. Heyerdahl listened to the current as the waves hit the shore on the island. Although accepted theories assumed that the Polynesians' ancestors had sailed there from Asia, Heyerdahl noticed all the connections with South America in the ocean currents, food, statues, and local origin myths.

When scientists argued that no South American people could have reached Polynesia with their "primitive" watercraft, Heyerdahl answered with his famous *Kon Tiki* voyage. In 1947 he built a balsa raft in the style of the Incas, basically a log raft held together only by ropes and wooden pegs, and with five companions left from Peru. In 101 days he covered 5,000 miles and reached the Raroia Atoll in Polynesia. Without proving that it did happen long ago, Heyerdahl proved that such a migration was possible.

Heyerdahl made other types of prehistoric boats and took long voyages with them. He traveled on papyrus reed boats, *Ra* and *Ra II*, from North Africa to the Caribbean in 1969 and 1970. In 1978 he sailed from the Middle East to Asia to Africa and back on an Iraqi reed boat. All these voyages attempted to demonstrate links among major early civilizations. Heyerdahl believes the world's oceans have served as highways for humankind ever since the first boats were built—not a strange idea for a Norwegian to have!

Heyerdahl sailed his reed boats under the United Nations flag with a multinational crew to show that peaceful coexistence under extreme conditions is possible. He was also the first to warn the United Nations about the pollution of the world's oceans.

Debating the Future

As a nation Norway seems to contain many paradoxes. Norwegians consider themselves modern, but they get married in traditional national costumes. Norway has one of the highest standards of living in the world, but most people eat lunch from brown paper bags and eat simple food—heavy on the potatoes—at home. Most Norwegians believe NATO has made Norway more secure, and yet a film such as *Orion's Belt* (1985) was very popular: Set off of Svalbard, the film dramatized how citizens become human pawns in intrigues between NATO members and the Soviet Union. Norwegian values stress both collective organization and deep-rooted individualism.

Most of the seeming paradoxes reflect the realities of a small country that has gone through tremendous changes in the past century. One American historian, Franklin D. Scott, has suggested that everything about Norway has changed "except for the continuing importance of

Emigration to America

Though some Norwegians had emigrated to the early colonies in North America, the real beginnings of Norwegian emigration date from 1825, when the tiny sloop *Restauration* (one quarter the tonnage of the *Mayflower*) carried fifty-two Norwegians from Stavanger to New York.

They were the first in what became a growing flood of emigrants from Norway from 1840 to World War I. While the first group included some Norwegians who had been converted to Quakerism in England, where they were taken as prisoners during the Napoleonic Wars, most left because of rural poverty. They left behind small cottages that have been called "starvation cottages." Many had been farm laborers who were paid only a few pennies a day or children of farmers whose plots were too small or unfertile to support an extended family.

Altogether more than 800,000 Norwegians emigrated to the United States before the U.S. Immigration Act of 1924 restricted the flow. The peak year was 1882, when 28,668 migrated. A larger percentage of the native population emigrated to the United States from Norway than from any other country except Ireland.

Life was never very easy for those who settled in mostly farming communities in the Midwest, New York, and California. Norwegian-language newspapers, churches, and voluntary associations helped knit the communities together. Some returned after a few years and found the situation in Norway had improved.

The bonds between Norway and the United States have been strengthened by a number of societies on both sides of the Atlantic, and both public and private organizations aid Americans interested in researching their family genealogies. Today there are nearly as many people of Norwegian descent living in the United States as there are Norwegians in Norway.

the merchant fleet and the magnificence of her mountains." Until after World War II there were still some Norwegians who thought about emigrating to America in order to live better. Now there are elderly Norwegian-born Americans who think about returning to Norway to have better social services.

Treholt/Traitor

Norwegians see themselves as strong individuals and are not shocked by their political differences and disagreements. But in spite of their respect for individualism, Norwegians were uniformly shocked when Arne Treholt, a high-ranking Labor Party official and a senior diplomat, was arrested, tried, and convicted in 1985 for spying for the Soviet KGB for nearly ten years. When he was arrested by Norwegian Security Police in January 1984, they found 832 secret documents in his apartment. He had also spied to a lesser extent for Iraq.

Treholt had been a member of the Norwegian mission to the United Nations, and previously a junior minister with the Ministry of Trade when Norway was negotiating with the Soviet Union about boundaries in the Barents Sea. Though he was not the first Norwegian to spy for the KGB, his high position made his actions more upsetting. Attempts to understand his behavior abound—in the thoughts of his former colleagues, in his own best-selling book, *Alone* (1986), written in jail, and in the book by his wife, Kari Storaekre, *God Tur Til Paris* (*Have a Nice Trip to Paris*, 1985).

Norwegians had felt that such high-level betrayal was not possible in their land. Quisling was a traitor whose actions everyone knew about. With Treholt, the belief that Norway was a close-knit society in which citizens could openly disagree but still trust each other was seriously challenged.

Treholt received the maximum sentence—in a society where no

crime now gets more than twenty-one years. The Norwegian criminal justice system is comparatively lenient by international standards in line with the Norwegians' attitude that they are all part of the same community and must live together.

EC/Yes or EC/No

How closely Norway should be tied to the rest of Europe is also a troubling issue for Norwegians. The discussion has gone on since 1961, when Britain, Norway's major trade partner and a co-member in the European Free Trade Association (EFTA), applied to join the European Economic Community. In 1970 Norway sent in a formal application, and negotiations were completed by January 1972.

Before making its decision, the Storting and the cabinet had promised to hold a national advisory referendum. Seventy-eight percent of eligible voters participated in the vote in September 1972. A majority of 53.5 percent voted "no" to membership. Although the referendum was not legally binding, it was accepted, and the government, which had strongly supported joining the EEC, resigned.

The vote against membership in the Common Market (which has since broadened into the European Community, EC) surprised many in Norway and in the rest of Europe. How could those who were pro-market have failed? The manufacturers association was pro-market; most of the work force was pro-market; the major newspapers were pro-market; leaders of the two major parties (Conservative and Labor) and the majority of the Storting were pro-market; the majority of bureaucrats were pro-market; in the towns 56.2 percent of the voters were pro-market.

The reason the pro-market coalition failed can be found in the strength of a "red-green" alliance, as it has been called. This alliance also is a cross-section of Norwegian opinions. The "red-green" link was between radical socialists, on the one hand, and farmers and fishers, who felt threatened by the possibility of a removal of state subsidies that have existed in some form since soon after World War I. The chairman of the Norwegian Milk Manufacturers' Federation was the founder of the People's Movement Against Norwegian Membership in the EEC, which had a good-sized budget and an effective organization. Slogans argued for national sovereignty and the preservation of the rural way of life and against the economic system of the EEC.

Sixty-two percent in the countryside voted no, but the percentage was over 71 percent in the three northern counties where fishing is most important. Many traditional Protestants were concerned about the importance of Catholicism in southern Europe, and voted no. Some of the no voters were also advocates of Nynorsk who felt Norway has not been independent long enough to be ready to give up its own decision making.

Another group of no voters was quite different: anticapitalists, ecology activists, urban intellectuals, and student radicals who were against any large common market where principles of "big business" would dominate. Still others, especially those who had lived through World War II, resisted the idea of being in a union with Germany. Even today the word "union" is a "bad" word in Norway because the country was not an equal partner in its union with Denmark (1380–1814) or with Sweden (1814–1905).

The EEC issue brought out the divisions that have long existed in Norway and that are still there today: the general tension between a concern to preserve much of Norwegian traditional life and a concern to integrate Norway more fully into the international community. The 1972 debate was the most heated that Norway has ever seen. For at least fifteen years Norwegians shied away from further discussion.

The question of whether to join the European Community remains and must be faced. Many government officials predict that Norway will, in fact, join the EC in the 1990's. In late 1990 Norway linked its currency, the krone, to the European Currency Unit (ECU). Many businesses already deal with customers in EC countries as they would if Norway were a member. However, Norway's history and its different interest groups, which reflect that history, could wind up supporting either ending: EC/Yes or EC/No.

Norway will probably do rather well either way, though the emphasis on oil and gas in recent years has left older industries with old problems and with fewer young executives and inventive personnel to confront them. The decision will again involve a referendum allowing all voters to be heard.

The Road to the Olympic Games

The thought that Lillehammer could host the Winter Olympic Games began as a "wild idea" in 1981 that initially met with disbelief. When Crown Prince Harald (now King) was first told of the idea, his reply was: "You must be kidding!"

The town of Lillehammer's coat of arms portrays a Birkebeiner skier. Municipality of Lillehammer

The range of later reactions reflected the normal divisions in Norway. Local business people stressed that Lillehammer had stable weather conditions, sports facilities nearby that could be expanded, and experience in arranging sports events. Most agreed that if done well, the Winter Olympics could stimulate trade, industry, and tourism and provide new employment opportunities in an inland area.

But others asked: Was such a huge undertaking financially feasible? Wasn't it a handicap that Lillehammer was virtually unknown internationally? Environmentalists were concerned that the Games would disturb the area's ambience and natural setting. One local leader of the Socialist Left Party described the Games as "a golden castle in the sky . . . Who needs that? We need to develop our country sensibly and steadily."

As support from the King, the Ministry of Industry, the Ministry of Foreign Affairs, and others grew, it was decided, in the spirit of "The Woman Against the Stream," to fight stubbornly against the odds and to fight well. Soon an audiovisual program, "The Challenge," was produced stressing Norway's accomplishments in the oil industry in the difficult environment of the North Sea, with the message that if a nation could manage this, it could certainly arrange perfect Olympic Winter Games.

As time went on, it became clear that a bid for the Winter Olympics was a feat of international diplomacy. Lillehammer did not win in its first bid, but the reaction of those closest to the project was: "Good. We will be far better equipped to make a bid for 1994."

By the next round Prime Minister Gro Harlem Brundtland had written to all the International Olympic Committee members, promising that Norway would mobilize all its resources so that Lillehammer would be the right place for the Winter Games. Work began on various

Norwegians always find a way to maintain their special ties to nature.   Ola Røe

new winter sports arenas. Research was done on why committee members had voted against Lillehammer earlier, so that misconceptions about Lillehammer as "a little town in a cold, inhospitable country" could be challenged.

The International Olympics Committee met in Seoul, Korea, in 1988 to select the location of the 1994 Winter Games, and the Norwegians watched as the competition narrowed down to the proposals from Sweden and Norway. The King of Sweden was there to lead Sweden's marketing program, but Gro Harlem Brundtland made a very strong impression in her final speech, dealing with sports medicine, ecology, and the role of the Olympics and Norway in world peace.

When the announcement came, "The decision is Lillehammer," there were still newspapers that had difficulty pinpointing Lillehammer on the map. A Korean newspaper placed the town deep in the heart of Sweden. But the town of Lillehammer rejoiced that they had outdone the Swedes and set about to show that Norway could be a proper host to the entire world.

As Norway looks to the twenty-first century, debates on issues like the EC, ecology, and oil revenues may at times accent differences of opinion, but Norwegians will also be united by their long-standing shared values that stress the rule of law, humanitarianism, and social equality.

Bibliography

Note: Most of the books included here have been written for a general audience, sometimes for visitors to Norway, and are not highly technical. Those which have been written specifically for younger readers are marked with an asterisk.*

A. General

Bryne, Arvid, and Joan Henriksen. *Norway Behind the Scenery*. Oslo: J. W. Cappelens, 1986. An interesting dialogue between a Norwegian and an American living in Norway that covers many topics in a chatty way.

Facts About Norway. Oslo: Schbsted, 1990. An informative, up-to-date, and easy-to-read handbook.

Popperwell, Ronald G. *Norway*. New York: Praeger, 1972. An authoritative study covering history, politics, economics, and art. For the serious student.

Sather, Leland B. *Norway*. Santa Barbara, Calif.: Clio Press, 1986. An extensive annotated bibliography of books in English for all ages.

Scott, Franklin D. *Scandinavia*. Cambridge, Mass.: Harvard University Press, 1975. Some interesting comparative generalizations about each country separately and as a region, as well as a chapter on Scandinavian Americans.

Segelcke, Nanna. *Made in Norway*. Oslo: Dreyer's Forlag, 1990. An interesting account of Norwegian inventions and specialties, from the paper clip and cheese slicer to knitting styles and antique farm furniture.

Selby, Arne. *Norway Today: An Introduction to Modern Norwegian Society*. Oslo: Norwegian University Press, 1986. Distributed by Oxford University Press. A general textbook on Norwegian society in the 1980's by a sociologist born in Oslo, educated in Norway and the United States, and currently teaching in the United States.

B. Top of Europe
(Chapters I, III, IV, and V)

Arlov, Thor B. *A Short History of Svalbard*. Oslo: Norsk Polarinstitutt, 1989. A short handbook with historic photos and extensive bibliography.

John, Brian Stephen. *Scandinavia: A New Geography*. New York: Longman, Green & Co., Inc., 1981; London: Longman Group Ltd., 1984. A solid general social geography text on all five Scandinavian countries: Denmark, Finland, Iceland, Sweden, and Norway.

Mead, W. R. *The Scandinavian Northlands*. Problem Regions of Europe series. London: Oxford University Press, 1974. Deals with the special situation of the Arctic areas in Norway, Sweden, and Finland in a short account.

C. The People (Chapter II)

Hagen, Anders. *Norway*. Ancient Peoples and Places series. New York: Praeger, 1967. Although not recent, still the best basic introduction to Norwegian prehistory.

Sami Instituhtta. *The Sami People*. Karasjok, Norway: Davvi Giri O.S., 1990. A comprehensive introduction to the history and current social organization of the Sami in northern Scandinavia, with a special emphasis on Norway.

D. History (Chapters VI–XI)

Abrahamsen, Samuel. *Norway's Response to the Holocaust: A Historical Perspective*. New York: Holocaust Library, 1991. A thoroughly researched account of Norwegian Jews and their wartime fate.

Andenaes, Johs, et al. *Norway and the Second World War*, 4th ed. Oslo: Aschehoug, 1989. Gives the background on all major events, including the controversy surrounding the trial of Quisling.

Derry, T. K. *A History of Scandinavia*. Minneapolis: University of Minnesota Press, 1979. A solid history of the Scandinavian countries from the earliest times to the present day, intended for readers who have little prior knowledge of Scandinavia.

Jesch, Judith. *Women in the Viking Age*. Rochester, NY: Boydell Press, 1991. The first book-length study in English to look at what women did in the Viking Age, both at home and in Scandinavia, on Viking expeditions, and in the Viking colonies from Greenland to Russia.

Lovoll, Odd S. *The Promise of America: A History of the Norwegian-American People*. Oslo: Universitetsforlaget, 1984. Distributed in the United States by University of Minnesota Press. An account of the Norwegian immigrants and the growth of an ethnic subculture in America.

*Magnusson, Magnus. *Viking Expansion Westwards*. New York: Henry Z. Walck, Inc., 1973. A lively account of the achievements of the Norwegians, including sailing to North America.

Prytz, Kåre. *Westward Before Columbus*. Oslo: Norsk Maritimt Forlag, 1991. Gives many little-known facts about extensive Viking activities in North America during the five hundred years before Columbus arrived.

*Taylor, Paul B., and W. H. Auden, trans. *The Elder Edda: A Selection*. New York: Random House, 1967. A good introduction to Norse mythology.

E. Democratic Traditions, Government, and Holidays (Chapters XII–XIV)

Greve, Tim. *Haakon VII of Norway: The Man and the Monarch*. New York: Hippocrene Books, Inc., 1983. A biography of Norway's first modern king from his early years in Denmark through fifty-two years as King.

Haavio-Mannila, Elina, et al. *Unfinished Democracy: Women in Nordic Politics*. New York: Pergamon Press, 1985. A collection of essays by Scandinavian feminists active in political affairs.

Henriksen, Vera. *Christmas in Norway: Past and Present*. Oslo: Aschehoug, 1970. Old and new customs in the celebration of Christmas.

Heyerdahl, Thor. "Norway in the World," in Knut Ramberg, ed., *Destination Lillehammer*. Oslo: J. M. Stenersens Forlag, A.S., 1989.

G. Literature, Art, and Music

Benestad, Finn, and Dag Schjelderup-Ebbe. *Edvard Grieg: The Man and the Artist.* Lincoln, Neb.: University of Nebraska Press, 1989. An extensive and authoritative biography looking at Grieg's life and career in the context of his times.

Benkow, Jo. *Fra Synagogen til Løvebakken (From the Synagogue to the Lion's Hill).* Oslo: Gyldendal Norsk Forlag, 1985. Not yet translated.

Beyer, Edvard. *Ibsen: The Man and His Work.* London: Souvenir Press, 1978. A critical study of Ibsen and his literary works, including contemporary cartoons, photographs of performances of Ibsen's works, and an extensive bibliography.

Boe, Alf. *Edvard Munch.* New York: Rizzoli, 1989. An extensive account of the life and work of Norway's major painter, by the director of the Munch Museum in Oslo.

Brunsdal, Mitzi. *Sigrid Undset: Chronicler of Norway.* New York: St. Martin's Press, 1989. A new biography of Undset's life and assessment of her major works.

Grøndahl, Carl Henrik, and Nina Tjomsland. *The Literary Masters of Norway.* Oslo: Tanum-Norli, 1978. Contains lively sketches and short excerpts from nine major authors.

Hanson, Katherine, ed. *An Everyday Story: Norwegian Women's Fiction.* Seattle: Seal Press, 1983. Includes stories from over twenty writers from the past to the present.

Svendsen, Kari B., trans. *Tales of the Norsemen.* Oslo: Gyldendal Norsk Forlag, 1985. Fourteen folktales retold in modern English by a Norwegian-American writer and journalist. Includes "The Woman Against the Stream" under the title of "The Contradictory Wife."

Norwegian literary historians used to talk about *de fire store* (The Big Four): Ibsen, Bjørnson, Lie, and Kielland, but there are many other noteworthy authors. The advanced student interested in looking at the diversity of Norwegian literature, including working-class historical novels by Johan Falkberget (1879–1967) and a Landsmål writer such as Arne Garborg (1851–1924), a poor farmer's son, should look at: Sven H. Rossel, *A History of Scandinavian Literature: 1870–1980* (Minneapolis: University of Minnesota Press, 1982) for a bibliography.

H. Sports and Explorers

Heyerdahl, Thor. *Easter Island: The Mystery Solved.* New York: Random House, 1989. Most libraries have several books by Heyerdahl, who has written numerous books and articles about his many adventures.

Kleppen, Halvor. *Telemark Skiing: Norway's Gift to the World.* Oslo: Det Norske Samlaget, 1986. A history of skiing in Norway and to a lesser extent in Europe and the United States (where telemarking has had a comeback), with many photos and interesting quotations.

*Miller, Margaret J. *Roald Amundsen: First to the South Pole.* London: Hodder & Stoughton, 1981. A biography of Amundsen discussing his entire career, as well as his journey to the South Pole.

*Noel-Baker, Francis. *Fridtjof Nansen: Arctic Explorer.* Lives to Remember. London: Adam & Charles Black. 1958. A brief biography of Fridtjof Nansen as Arctic explorer, Norwegian statesman, and humanitarian.

Waitz, Grete, and Gloria Averbuch. *World Class.* New York: Warner Books, 1986. A blend of autobiography and running advice.

I. Magazines and Pamphlets

NORINFORM produces *Norway Now*, a monthly review of current events, which may be ordered from: Norway Now, P.O. Box 241, Sentrum, N-0103, Oslo 1, Norway for a fee. Other pamphlets are available from the Norwegian Information Service, 825 Third Avenue, New York, N.Y. 10022. A popular pamphlet is "How to Trace Your Ancestors in Norway," by Yngve Nedrebø.

Scandinavian Review, published four times a year by the American-Scandinavian Foundation, 725 Park Avenue, New York, N.Y. 10021, has nicely written, interesting articles.

Filmography

Norway has a small subsidized film industry. Annual catalogues are available from The Norwegian Film Institute, P.O. Box 482, Sentrum, N-0105, Oslo 1, Norway. The Norwegian Film Festival is held in Haugesund every summer.

The Norwegian Information Service has some films and video, for free loan. Available 16-mm. films include:

Crescendo. 1985. 15 min. A documentary on Oslo showing everyday life during each of the four seasons. (Also in video.)

Cycle of Life. 1974. 15 min. Norwegian music as background to views of sculptures by Norwegian sculptor Gustav Vigeland.

Norwegian Landscapes. 1983. 27 min. A presentation of Norway's magnificent nature and people during all seasons. (Also in video.)

Videos include *Oslo Alive!* (26 min.; 1987); *Grieg Fantasies* (21 min.; 1987); *Norway—An Oil and Gas Nation* (17 min.; 1988); *Norde* (15 min.; 1989); *Rooms with a View* (16 min.; 1990); and *Norwegian Notes* (24 min.; 1989). These videos and the short films may be borrowed from: Audience Planners, Inc., 5107 Douglas Fir Road, Calabasa, Calif. 91302. Photos by Ola Røe may be ordered from: Ola Røe, Røe Foto, AS, P.O. Box 528, 900l Tromsø, Norway.

Index

Numbers in *italics* refer to illustrations.